BIGGER

Is

BETTER

BIGGER

Is

BETTER

Real-Life Wisdom

from the

No-Drama Mama

Big Ang

x

Gallery Books

New York   London   Toronto   Sydney   New Delhi

Gallery Books
Division of Simon & Schuster, Inc.
1230 Avenue of the Americas
New York, NY 10020

First Gallery Books hardcover edition September 2012

GALLERY BOOKS and colophon are registered trademarks
of Simon & Schuster, Inc.

For information about special discounts for bulk purchases,
please contact Simon & Schuster Special Sales at 1-866-506-1949
or business@simonandschuster.com.

The Simon & Schuster Speakers Bureau can bring authors to your
live event. For more information or to book an event contact the
Simon & Schuster Speakers Bureau at 1-866-248-3049 or visit
our website at www.simonspeakers.com.

Designed by Jason Snyder

Manufactured in the United States of America

1 3 5 7 9 10 8 6 4 2

Library of Congress Cataloging-in-Publication Data is available.

ISBN: 978-1-4516-9961-6
ISBN: 978-1-4516-9962-3(ebook)

To my grandson, my heart,
my soul, the air that I breathe.
I love you, my boy, Baby Sal.
xoxo

CONTENTS

CONTENTS

CONTENTS

ix

HOW TO LIVE BIG

*N*ine years ago, I was under house arrest for a drug conviction. Two years ago, I was $100,000 in debt. And now, I'm about to move into a mansion, I'm on TV, and people from Saudi Arabia come to my bar to meet me. It's hard not to look at life's changing circumstances and realize you control only two things:

1. Your style

2. How you treat other people

I don't want to look back on my life and think, "Man, was I a toxic bitch." I want to think, "Everyone loved me. My style was fabulous. I had a big heart." I want to live large.

Living Large means surrounding yourself with family and friends, cooking with bold flavors, dressing loud and proud, making a million crazy mistakes and then *getting over it*. It's about staying young—in how you look and how you feel—and laughing, hard and often. I'm known for my laugh, which some fans have compared to Herman Munster's. When I think something is funny, you'll know it: my jaw drops, my mouth opens, and a big gust bursts out that makes my whole body shake. When I throw a party, it's a blowout. Diamonds? Of course, bigger is better! When I go on vacation, it's first-class all the way. If I'm having one person over for dinner, I cook for ten. You never know if more people are going to drop by. When they do, they'll be hungry.

Small is not how I do things. The only small thing in my life is my Pomeranian, Little Louie. Even though he's just two pounds, he still makes a big statement. To me, the small life is staying home every night alone. It's wearing all-black clothes that go up the neck. It's eating a turkey sandwich on dry toast for lunch every day. It's being afraid to take risks, and thinking that the best days of your life are behind you.

Because of my large life, people react to me in a big way. I've heard it again and again: "Everyone loves Big Ang." I'd deny it, but that'd be false modesty, and I don't do false (except for implants and eyelash extensions). Everyone *does* love me. Put a baby in my lap, he stops crying and starts drooling. Put an old man in my lap, same thing. Even before I got famous, I'd walk into a club and people would flock to my side. My house is the most popular on the block. People come to my bar, the Drunken Monkey, and they just don't want to leave.

As for *why* people love me, it's not so hard to understand.

They know I'll try to make them laugh. I'm not going to throw a punch. A hot dish and a cold drink will appear before them within minutes. I treat people with respect, and I don't do drama. I just want everyone to have a good time and be happy.

Maybe I try to inspire happiness because I know how it feels to be seriously miserable. I've had my share of hard times—including an early divorce and rocky second marriage, health problems, both my parents dying too young, raising kids alone, going broke, getting arrested, watching loved ones sent to prison and fall to cancer. Those low points have made me realize the only things that matter are family, friends, and health. Plus a diamond bracelet, a fur coat, a good haircut, a glass of cabernet, and a plate of steak pizzaiola. Just give me those, along with my self-respect, and I can get through anything.

This book isn't to say "Do what I do" or "It's my way or the Staten Island Expressway." For the scores of rules in this book, there's one that rules them all: "Rules are meant to be broken." I've made a ton of mistakes in my life (although I regret *nothing*). But who am I to give advice? I don't judge anyone or tell other people how to live. That's not my style. What you'll find here are just things I've done, how I've got through bad times and good, what makes me smile (e.g., puppies and diamonds), and what makes me roll my eyes (e.g., bargain-basement plastic surgeons and cheating rat bastards).

BIG ANG

One thing to know about me right away: my door is always open. Usually half a dozen or more people are around my kitchen table, having a bite to eat, telling their stories and neighborhood news. It's loud and crazy, and that's how I like it. So before you go any further, open a bottle, pour a nice drink, and *then* turn the page. *Salute!*

PART 1

STYLE

STYLE IS BIGGER THAN JUST WHAT I WEAR
and how I blow out my hair. It's the way I burst into a
bangin' club. It's how I roll, literally, down the highway
in my Jag or in a Winnebago on vacation. Style is an
attitude, a swagger. It's how I think, drink, talk, walk,
and *laugh*. Everything I put on—from hair extensions
to nail tips, wallpaper to disco tunes—I do for a reason.
It expresses my personality and defines sexy as I see it.

My relationships are the greatest gift of my life.
But style is how I present my life in a big, beautiful box
with glittering gold wrapping.

1
Big Beauty Rules

You can't control that much in life. Bad things happen. Accidents. Arrests. Problems hit you out of nowhere. But hair? That's one thing we can (usually) rely on. It's a comfort to know that you can do something small—a mani-pedi, a blowout—and feel a whole lot better about life, no matter what's going on outside the salon. I'm not saying beauty treatments will make your mortgage payments disappear or turn your no-good husband into a prince. But even in a big life, the little things help a lot. When you look good, you feel good. I don't know any woman on earth who'd deny that essential truth.

ALWAYS HAVE A TAN

Even in the dead of winter, I have a tan. I just don't feel right without it. When my skin gets a little bit pale, it feels like I'm walking around completely naked—and not in a good way.

In the bedroom of one of my former houses, I had a full-size tanning bed set up next to the regular bed. I called it the *beds*room. The tanning bed, a gift from my baby sister, Janine, was a huge apparatus with long tubes on the top lid and a bottom platform where you lay down. I'd stretch out on it—completely nude; who wants tan lines?—every night for a few minutes. It was my peaceful time to myself.

If I hadn't used it, I would probably be dead now from vitamin D deficiency. Most people take natural sunlight for granted. They're out there, soaking it up like human sponges, just doing their daily business. Bartenders like me, who start the day in the middle of the afternoon and don't go to bed until dawn, just don't get enough sunshine. That's why I called my old bar Nocturnals, for all the creatures of the night, like me. How funny that everyone who went there had deep dark tans! I love my vacations in the tropics. But you can't cram an entire year's worth of sun exposure into a couple of weeks in Aruba.

So I adored the tanning bed . . . until I started dreading it. Claustrophobia hit me out of nowhere. Whenever I closed myself into that contraption, I'd feel anxious. When I was younger, I wasn't afraid of anything. I'd ride the Cyclone at

Coney Island all day long. The roller-coaster experience—the dips, jolts, and turns—used to be fun. I enjoyed feeling out of control. But now, at fifty-two, I never go on amusement park rides anymore. I don't want to feel upside down, belly churning like crazy. If I want thrills nowadays, I . . . well, actually, I don't want them. Now, I want calm. It's enough for me to just get through the week in one piece. I came to hate closing myself into that coffinlike tanning bed. So I gave it to my cousin Sallyann, and she keeps it in her garage.

So now, I get a spray tan at the salon a couple of times a month. I go into a stall, like a shower, and a few nozzles blast bronzer at my body from top to bottom, front and back. On an episode of *Mob Wives*, a girl set up a temporary tanning booth at my house. My castmate Drita and I put on our bikinis and got sprayed. It was great because when a professional applies the stuff, you get an even all-over tan, including the tricky spots like the armpits and the underboob area. The worst is when you do the automatic booth and miss a huge patch, or your face gets nut brown and your neck is white as glue.

IT'S ALL ABOUT THE HAIR

My hair always looks good. My girl Tina—aka the Chinese Big Ang—at Beyond Beauty salon in Staten Island does my blowouts a couple of times a week. My hair has a natural wave to it, but I prefer it stick straight. I've tried to straighten it myself, but I do a lousy job. I don't even own a hair dryer or a flat iron.

One of the reasons I don't exercise: if I sweat, I'll ruin my blowout.

I've experimented with haircuts and color over the years. I've had bangs on and off. I love, love, love superlong extensions, in black and in every color of the rainbow. I've been blond a few times. I think every woman should mix it up by going blond at least once in her life, if only with a decent wig. You put on a new head of hair and feel like a new woman. Instant cure for boredom.

Early on in my pregnancy with my son, A.J., I decided I wanted to go blond. So I had my hair bleached and walked out of the salon with a gorgeous head of long blond hair and loved it. I went to bed and woke up bald. The hair fell out! I didn't know you're not supposed to dye your hair during the first trimester. There I was, pregnant, getting bigger every day, and bald as a rock.

Disaster.

For months, I wore hats. Cool hats. I rocked a fedora. But still.

Eventually, my hair did grow back in. For a time, though, it was supershort and white blond. This was 1989. New Wave was hot and I had perfect hair for it. I was right on trend, totally by accident.

" Ang can pull off any hairstyle in a big way. For my thirtieth birthday, she planned a party for me. Our crew went to the Short Hills Hilton for the night. At the time, she had really short blond hair. When we pulled up to the entrance of the hotel in a limo, people were looking in the windows, trying to see who it was. Ang stepped out the limo, tall and glamorous with the short blond hair. People were asking, 'Who is that?' We told everyone she was Brigitte Nielsen. They believed it and kept pushing in to get a picture with her."

—Sallyann, cousin

" When Ang had long blond hair, people on the street stopped her all the time thinking she was some celebrity or another. I remember going shopping with her, and a woman mistook Ang for Victoria Gotti. Ang is tall, and Victoria is petite. But it didn't matter. Ang always looks so great, everyone assumes she has to be someone famous."

—Rita, aunt

GO LONG OR GO LONGER

It takes two hours to put on my bling-bling nails. Time well spent. I get to relax and chat with Tina. I walk out of the salon with gorgeous square-shaped gel tips with two dozen individually attached rhinestones. The nails are long, of course, about two inches. I smile every time I look at them. It's a great trick to have to look no further than the backs of my hands to find shine and sparkle. Just doing boring, everyday things like dialing the phone or pouring a drink draws my attention to my elegant nails, and I instantly feel like a glamazon.

Only drawback: it is hard to chop garlic.

❝ Angela has been coming to my salon for five years, and we've formed a very good friendship. She's been a big part of my salon's success. She helped me get more and more customers as the years went by, by telling everyone how much she loves my shop.

"I am an immigrant from China. Not once did Angela make a racist remark about me—you'd be surprised what people do say. I am so happy to be her friend. Quality friends are hard to come by."

—*Tina, owner of Beyond Beauty*

LASH OUT

What could be prettier than superlong, thick, dark eyelashes? I'm not a fan of false lashes, with the glue and having to peel them off. Instead, I get eyelash extensions—a fake lash is glued on to each of my own individual lashes, making them twice as long and thick. It takes a couple of hours to fill in every few weeks and it costs a fortune. But on the plus side, I never need mascara. Every flutter of my eyelids is like being in a movie from the sixties, when all the girls had huge lashes and big eyes. I find people staring at my lashes, trying to figure out what's going on there. I get a kick out of watching them react. First, the *Wow!* Then, a little confusion. And then, just awe.

> " Ang was always the first to try something new. Even as a teenager, she was the first to get waxed or get streaks in her hair. She always recommended people, too. 'I've got a great hair person,' she'd say, or, 'This is the best place to buy shoes.' She's not the kind of woman who keeps a great store or stylist to herself. She wants her friends to get in on her finds. And everyone does. Ang is a trendsetter."
>
> —Deb, "aunt"

NO SWEAT

Fans of *Mob Wives* remember when I bungled a belly dance with Karen and Ramona on the show. Ramona said that I couldn't do the moves because of my "beyond-enormous boobs." It was kind of a bitchy comment, but whatever. She might be right: My center of gravity is higher than a normal woman's. Gyrating my hips was exhausting! Never again. I do not see belly dancing in my future. Same goes for yoga, Zumba, Pilates—all that bouncy, bendy crap. Back in the eighties, I danced at Pastels, a famous disco in Bay Ridge, Brooklyn, for hours and never got tired. But that was then. Disco is dead, in case you haven't heard. (RIP Donna Summer.)

Nowadays, if I want exercise, I take Little Louie on long walks through Staten Island's Clove Lakes and Silver Lake Parks. I lift my three-year-old grandson, Sal, and chase after him. I stand for hours in heels while bartending at the Drunken Monkey, which keeps my calf, tummy, and butt muscles tight. But if it's not about my pets, my kids, or my work, I don't do traditional gym exercise. Self-torture is not part of my lifestyle.

Okay, once I hired a trainer. I was under house arrest at the time and figured, since I was stuck at home, I might as well try to get in shape. She came over every week and put me through the paces. Running in place. Lunges. Crunches. Push-ups. With my boobs? Ridiculous. I don't mean to knock my trainer. I loved her! But working out was horrible. As soon as my house arrest ended, so did our sessions.

My friend Margo got it in her head awhile ago that all our friends should get in shape together. She made a gym room in her house, with exercise machines, weights, music, and TVs, a whole setup. If you didn't show up at her place for the scheduled workout, you had to put money into a kitty. If you *did* show up, as incentive you could do a shot or have a cigarette break after every fifteen minutes of exercising. Well, you can guess what happened. For a while, we all showed when we were supposed to. We'd barely break a sweat, then we'd start drinking and smoking and call the workout done for the day. But even that got to be too much. So we'd just stuff the kitty every week for all the workouts we missed. Before long, it got to be a lot of money. We talked about what we were going to do with it. Since everyone had the same idea, it wasn't a tough decision: We splurged on a massive feast at one of our favorite restaurants. So much for getting in shape.

I've been thinking lately, though, that I should try again and join a gym, lift some weights, get Dieseled up. My daughter, Raquel, has decided to start running every day while the baby naps. She puts on shorts and sneakers and runs the three-mile loop around the park—twice. I get winded running my mouth. We'll see. If hitting the gym doesn't work out, there's always lipo.

IT'S WORTH IT

Whatever you do to look good is worth the time and money. I'm not saying everyone should have superlong nails or get eyelash extensions. But I do believe pampering yourself a few times a month forces you to relax, slow down, and make a necessary mental adjustment. You'll leave the salon feeling better than you did when you walked in, which will make you happier and more fun to be around. And that's what it's all about: Doing what you can to make yourself and the people you love feel good.

2

Big Tattoo Rules

Tattoos are addicting. After I got my first one, I just wanted to get more. They're called body art because they're beautiful, emotionally evocative, and intended to be viewed and admired, like a painting in a museum. Tats tell a story. Each of mine reminds me of a person or a time in my life that was special enough to turn into an indelible mark.

PUT IT IN INK

I wouldn't put it on my body unless I was 100 percent committed to the sentiment of the tattoo. My body is my history, and my tattoos tell the story of what I stand for and care about.

At last count, I have twelve of them:

1. OMERTÀ. In script, on the back of my neck. *Omertà* means "code of silence." It's about loyalty to your friends and family. I believe in and practice this code so strongly, I put it in ink. It's a part of me, forever.

2. RAQUEL. My daughter's name, on my right wrist.

3. A.J. My son's name, also on my right wrist.

4. SALVATORE. My beautiful grandson's name, on my left wrist.

5. A champagne bottle and strawberries. Symbols of celebration and love of life, on my neck.

6. A monkey swinging on a vine. Along my hip. I love monkeys, plus the vine covers up my tummy-tuck scar.

7. A rose. On my ankle. I got this when I was fourteen. It was homemade with a needle and some ink, not something I'd recommend.

8. A ladybug and cherries. On my toe. My sister Janine and I both have these. We got them done together when I was under house arrest after my plea bargain.

9. Lips. On my ass, as in "Kiss my . . ."

10. Rosary beads. So I never have to carry the real things. The tattoo goes all the way around my ankle.

11. A bee. On my shoulder. It's in memory of the day I got stung by a bee at the breast-cancer walk in Prospect Park, Brooklyn, with my best friend, Cari-Ann, who was a tattoo artist.

12. Pink ribbon. On my lower back, the symbol for breast-cancer awareness, in memory of Cari-Ann. It's one of the only tats on my body she didn't put there herself.

" Everyone in our family gets tattoos. Mom's friend Cari-Ann used to come to the house and do them for us. She gave me my first tattoo—a tribal on my leg—at sixteen. When Mom recently suggested we spend the afternoon getting tattoos together, I thought, 'Why not? Let's go.' We sat there for a couple of hours, talking the whole time. Nice day. I'd do it again, anytime. Just name the day, Mom."

—A.J., son

"Ang and I were hanging out at the Beach Club right around the time I turned twenty-one. She decided she wanted raw clams for dinner, so we went to Lundy's. Her friend Cari-Ann had a shop inside Lundy's. Ang said, 'Come on, let's get tattoos!' Then she had an idea. 'If you get a tattoo of my face, I'll pay for it,' she said. I was really close to Ang, and I wanted a tattoo, so I said yes.

"Cari-Ann drew the picture of Ang—she was wearing a hat with a braid on one side—right onto my stomach with me lying on the table. Over the years, I have had to explain to girls why I have a tattoo of my aunt. But I ended up marrying Raquel's best friend, who loves Ang. We all run in the same circles. And we all have a sense of humor about it. As my wife says, she loves looking at Ang when she goes down on me."

—*Ronnie, nephew*

IF YOU CAN'T TAKE THE HEAT, GET OUT OF THE TATTOO PARLOR

I don't count these for my running total, but I also have facial tattoos on my eyelids and lips. Getting the eyelids done was more painful than surgery.

Torture! Of the purest kind!

I had no idea what I was in for. I just thought it would be a great time-saver to have black lines permanently etched along my upper and lower lids. I wouldn't have to deal with smudging, smearing, having to put makeup on and take it off every day and night. I figured, in the long run, I'd probably save money on makeup, too. (I don't wear a lot of makeup in general. With my lash extensions and year-round tan, I don't need a lot of extra. Just some eye shadow and lip gloss, which I go through by the gallon.)

So I went in and had it done. It hurt *so much* that I couldn't take it. I only did one eye. I ran out of there like a Cyclops, in agony, hand over my left eye and crying with both of them. I had to build up my courage for an entire year before I had the right eye done. While I was in the chair, I also had him tattoo a liner around my lips. It hurt, but that time, I didn't bolt.

Progress!

66 Angela was fourteen when she got a tattoo of a butterfly on her groin. She told our mother it was temporary, that it would wash away. So Mom got out a Brillo pad and tried to scrub it off. It was in the scabbed-over stage, and when Mom scrubbed, it started bleeding. Angela was screaming. She had to confess it was real to get Mom to stop scrubbing.

"Ang was sent to her room. She turned on the lights and the radio, opened the window, and snuck out. When she came home later, though, the window was locked, the lights were off, and she was busted. Ang had to come in the front door. Oh my God, she was in so much trouble. She got a beating that night."

—*Janine, sister*

TATS ARE NOT ALWAYS FOREVER

I've had three tattoos removed, two by accident, and one on purpose.

About ten years ago, I went in for a tummy tuck to get rid of my pooch, that little roll of flab where I stored my extra cannolis. I was in the recovery room afterward, and the doctor came in and asked, "Who's Losah? The name on the tattoo? Is he here?"

Quick backstory: During the hot-and-heavy period with a certain boyfriend, I'll call him Losah, I had his name tattooed on my belly near my hip. The relationship ended not too long after the tattoo healed, and I was stuck with LOSAH in swirly letters on an intimate body part where I knew all future boyfriends would *not* appreciate seeing it.

This doctor had seen it and was asking about the man himself.

I said, "No! He's long gone."

"Well, so is the tattoo." As part of the procedure, the doc had to remove some of my skin, including the entire tattoo. Good riddance. I also lost the butterfly tattoo, which I wasn't as happy about. The recovery from the tummy tuck was the worst pain I've ever had, including childbirth. I couldn't stand upright. No words for the suffering. Horrible. I walked stooped over like a hunchback for weeks.

The only tattoo I removed on purpose was one that said BIG ANG on my leg. It was homemade. My friend used a needle to inject ink under my skin, just like they do in prison. I was thirteen at the time and loved that tattoo the way only a teenage girl can fall madly in love with something reckless and kind of stupid. I could've gotten hepatitis or worse. When I was twenty-seven, I had it removed by professionals—for $4,000.

Why pay so much? It was a tremendous amount for me at the time! Four grand in 1987 dollars would be like $20,000 today. I'd just had Raquel, and I got it in my head that I didn't want my daughter to know about my nickname. As if removing the tattoo would do it! Everyone called me Big Ang. The name was permanent. I couldn't spend $1 million to remove it from everyone's brain. Although I wavered for a while, I'm glad people still call me Big Ang. That's who I was at thirteen, and who I still am at fifty-two.

NEVER FORGET WHAT MATTERS MOST

Even the tats I lost are still with me, in my memory. That's the greatest power of tattoos. Not only do you have the tat itself to remind you of your commitments, but you also keep the memory of getting the tattoo, what was happening in your life at the time, like keeping a diary.

3
Big Plastic Surgery Rules

I hate having surgery—all kinds, not only the cosmetic stuff. I've had surgery on my bladder and my thyroid. I was in a car accident recently and had to have a piece of bone taken out of my hip and attached to my neck with screws and a metal disk. Next time I go visit relatives in prison, I'm going to set off the metal detector, for sure.

It might seem like a contradiction, how much I hate surgery, and yet I've elected to have so much of it. It gets harder each time. I start to obsess about "What if they put me under, and I don't wake up?" When I was younger, I never worried like this. Now, I freak out. I always take something to calm me down before I go into the operating room. (Ideally, I'd be knocked out cold before I even arrive at the hospital.)

I try to focus on the result. With plastic surgery, the goal is looking young and sexy. Aging gracefully? What the hell is that about? I don't even know what it means. Why is it "graceful" to look old and decrepit with wrinkles, gray hair, and loose neck skin? The tools are out there, and I'm committed to using them.

" Ang's heart is so big, she had to get those big boobs to make room."

—Angelina, friend

GO BIG OR GO BIGGER

The first thing people notice when they meet me is the color of my eyes.

Yeah, right.

It's the boobs—then the lips, then back to the boobs. They're size 36J (*J* is for "jumbo"). It'll come as no surprise to anyone that they weren't always *this* enormous, but they have been substantial since they first sprang out of my chest. At fourteen, I was already a 36DD. The only drawback of having such large breasts? I can't sleep on my stomach. Who cares? Small price to pay.

My first augmentation was in 1985. I was twenty-five years old. During pregnancy and right after giving birth to Raquel, my tits inflated and got huge. I mean, HUGE—size 42J, like I was smuggling a pair of beach balls under my shirt. Maybe they wouldn't have blown up so much if I breast-fed. But that wasn't for me. It seemed like something animals do. So a couple of months after they inflated, they deflated—and sagged down to my waist. They looked like flattened watermelons. I could've tucked them into my jeans. It was gross.

During the mid-eighties, sponges were the best implants at the time, so that's what I had done. My boobs were round again and higher than before—which was great because I didn't want to be playing soccer with them before the age of thirty. I loved the look.

The doctors told me I should have the implants changed every decade. So in 1995, I went back in. By then, the implant of the moment was saline bags. Out went the sponges, and in came the saline. This time, I went bigger by a couple of sizes. I had them redone one more time, in 2005. Just keeping up with medical advances, I swapped the saline implants for silicone, threw in a boob lift (I was forty-five by then; gravity had taken its toll), and went up another couple of sizes to my current 36J. The scars have faded, and now you can barely see them at all. It's just a faint, superthin outline. I'm grateful for having naturally dark skin that heals well.

Three times is enough, though. I'm not going to go any

bigger. The size now is perfect. Guys love them—straight (obviously) and gay. On Gay Night at the Drunken Monkey, my bar in Staten Island, gay men come to see me and shove money between my tits. It's like my cleavage is the tollbooth to get on the Verrazano Bridge.

I wear Victoria's Secret unlined Body by Victoria DDs. Cups that small don't cover much. They're tit hammocks. It's not like I need a bra for support anyway. When I go commando, they don't budge. I could bend forward, to the side. If I could do a cartwheel, they would not move. They feel . . . firm. Not rock-solid cement balls like the horror stories you hear about implants gone wrong. But, compared to mushy normal boobs, they're pretty hard.

A few years ago, I was on vacation with my family at the Villa Roma resort in the Catskills. We were standing outside the restaurant when it turned from dusk to dark. Suddenly, the sky was full of bats. Now, I adore all animals, with the exception of rodents—especially rats, and their winged equivalent, bats. I don't get scared about walking home at 4:00 a.m. in six-inch heels in August through Bay Ridge, Brooklyn, but I'm deathly afraid of bats. So this resort was apparently bat heaven, and they were swarming all over the place. Out of nowhere, this bat flew right into my chest. Bam, he hit hard, then fell *splat* on the ground. We were all screaming and freaking out. The bat didn't move. We thought it was stunned. Turned out, he died on impact. My implants broke its little neck.

So when I say I have killer boobs, I freakin' mean it.

"I went to a Catholic school. I'd see the other mothers, and I knew Mom was different. Yeah, the boobs were a little embarrassing. People used to stare at her when she'd pick me up. I asked her to wear turtlenecks when she came for PTA conferences. When the principal, a priest, saw her for the first time, his eyes bugged out of his head. The poor guy probably had to give himself confession every day for a month."

—*Raquel, daughter*

READ MY LIPS (FROM SPACE)

I always thought my lips were too thin. Barely there lips are for dried-up old ladies. Big, juicy, puffy lips are sexy, and men love them. So, eleven years ago, I went out and got me some.

The doctor warned me that after he injected the collagen my lips would be really puffy at first, then they'd settle down after a few weeks. The strategy was to do a little more than you wanted, then wait for them to shrink into the desired shape and size, which, for me, was BIG. I wanted to make a sensational impact, and only juicy, over-the-top lips would do. Most people go in and get one or two tubes of the collagen injected.

I got five.

For the first few weeks, my lips looked like they'd been bee-stung *by the whole freakin' hive.* They were so swollen, I couldn't close my mouth. I had to drink with my head tilted up not to drool. In hindsight, it's kind of funny. At the time, though, I was so not laughing. Maybe I would have, but my lips were too stretched. If I cracked a smile, they might've exploded.

They did settle down. I was told that I'd have to go back in every six months to a year for a refresher injection. But that didn't happen. They shrank to the size you see now and didn't lose any more volume. I don't know if it was because I had so much injected at once or what. It's been over a decade, and they haven't changed. I like to think that my lips were always meant to be this way, so they stayed.

It's a plastic surgery miracle.

ALWAYS TAKE SOMEONE WITH YOU TO SEE A DOCTOR

I have brain freezes whenever I go to see a doctor. I know I'm in the office and he's talking to me, but I can't remember what he's said. I've spent an hour in a doctor's office and had to go back the next day because I had no idea what we talked about. It's anxiety. When I'm scared, I go deaf. So whenever I have a doctor's consultation about any kind of procedure, I take someone with me. It's usually Janine. She takes excellent notes, which I can read later and understand what I've gotten myself into.

YOU GET WHAT YOU PAY FOR

In 1998, I was at the nail salon and heard about a doctor in the city who would do procedures on his patients, no money down. He had a payment plan. I might've considered the source—some random woman in the pedicure chair next to me. I should've checked the surgeon out. But I didn't. All I heard was "no money down." The lure of having stuff done without spending a dime up-front was too tempting.

So Cari-Ann and I went to see him in Manhattan. She

wanted to get dermabrasion on her face, and I wanted to get lipo. We walked into the guy's office, and the waiting room was packed with transvestites, who we assumed were going to have sex-change operations.

This gave us pause. But did we turn around and walk out? No! The doctor came out of the room, and he was this old, decrepit troll. My instincts were saying, "Run!" But by that point, I'd come into the city, I'd been thinking about how I'd look postlipo. I was there, and I was going to get the procedure. Cari-Ann felt the same way. So we did.

The. Horror.

We came out of the operating room like bloody monsters. Cari-Ann looked like she'd had her face removed. I was black-and-blue from my neck to my ass, lumpy and limping, leaking fluids. People saw us on the street and screamed.

We spent the night at the Mayfair Hotel near Central Park afterward, and when we left the room the next day, it looked like a murder had gone down. We thought we were going to be arrested! All those bloody towels and sheets. I pitied the housekeeper. Don't worry, we gave her a nice tip.

Later on, Cari-Ann and I tried to sue the butcher, but he went bankrupt and never showed up in court. He either died or fled the country. I hope all those transvestites came out of his office looking better than we did.

I learned my lesson. No more cheapo plastic surgery. The

next time I get something done, I'm not going to trust some stranger's referral. I'm going to be much more careful. And it won't come soon enough. I want to have my eyes done. And a slight face-lift. And get my neck tightened. I'd also like to lipo the love handles and around my bra. My sister found me a new doctor on Facebook. Hey, at least I can check the customer comments and reviews. If any of them say, "He's no doctor, he's a butcher," forget it.

WHEN DOCTORS SAY, "THIS WON'T HURT," THEY'RE FULL OF SHIT

Every time a doctor tells me a procedure won't hurt, I always believe him or her. It's a willful delusion. I wouldn't go through with the procedure otherwise.

Case in point: I got the Botox recently.

Nightmare!

I'd been thinking about getting injections for the wrinkles on my forehead and around my eyes for a while. I was really excited when Janine and I went in to do it. I told the doctor what I had in mind. She had a thick foreign accent, though, and I couldn't understand what she was saying until I heard, "It's like a little face-lift."

Ding, ding, ding. Those were the magic words that made my wallet open. I said, "I want that!"

Then the doctor whipped out a *huge* syringe with a two-inch needle. My jaw dropped at the sight of it. The doctor told me to relax, and she started shooting up my face.

"Little ouch here," she said. "Little pinch. It's a walk in the park."

Yeah, a walk in the park—*in hell*. She was killing me. Let me tell you, the Botox is no joke. It burns. I thought I was going to have a heart attack. I broke out in a sweat. I held my breath the whole time. If I weren't sitting down already, I would probably have fainted.

The ordeal took about five minutes, but it felt like forever. Beauty is hard work! The assistant put a mirror in my hand. I expected my face to be covered with red dots, with blood and swelling. But I was pleasantly surprised. I looked great! I wouldn't call it a "little face-lift," exactly, but the wrinkles were gone. My cheeks were plumped up. I looked ten years younger. The doc suggested I wait a week and see if I liked it. If so, I could come do more.

"Can I do more now?" I asked.

She seemed surprised. "Uh, sure."

She broke out a new needle.

NO PAIN, NO GAIN

I guess the pain of surgery and injections is kind of like child-birth. The joy afterward helps you forget the pain. I didn't think I'd forget the trauma of the Botox after only twenty seconds. But, like most things, once you know what to expect, it's not as scary the second time around. In this way, I realized, the Botox is also a lot like marriage.

4

Big Wardrobe Rules

On the days I'm just hanging around the house, cleaning and cooking, I wear a sweatshirt, track pants, and sneakers. But even dressed like a slob, my hair looks nice, and I'm pulled together. Otherwise, I wouldn't feel right. For me, style is deeper than just what you wear. I'm not an artist in the traditional sense. I don't paint or draw. But how I look and dress is one way I express my creativity. Every piece of clothing, be it a fur coat or a pair of earrings, represents me, shows my personality, and reflects my unique taste.

And, man, do I taste freakin' *great*.

" Some women take hours to get ready. For Ang, it's fifteen minutes and she's ready to go. And then she puts her attention on you. She always wants to help you with clothes and makeup, so you'll look perfect and feel great."

—Deb, "aunt"

DRESS LOUD AND PROUD

I love clothes! Everything I wear makes me feel sexy and confident. I owe it to my customers at the bar to look hot—especially on Gay Night! The gays have high expectations, and I'd hate to disappoint them. When they see me walking Little Louie through the park, or behind the bar, they break out into a smile. It makes me happy to make others happy. In this way, wearing the hell out of my clothes is like performing a public service.

> " I saw this hundred-year-old Chinese robe, hand stitched for an empress, at a store in Florida. It's a work of art as much as a piece of clothing. I fell in love with it and bought it. It was too long for me to wear—I'm only five feet three inches—so I hung it up on my wall at my house. I'd look at it every day, and think, 'This robe was made for Big Ang.' When she came to visit me I gave it to her. I knew she'd like it, but didn't know if she'd actually wear it. Immediately, she put it on. Well, it *was* made for her. With her height and hair, she looked like an empress herself. She said, 'I'm going to put on a pair of heels and wear it out.' No one else but Ang could pull it off."
>
> —Deb, "aunt"

STYLE STRATEGIES

Here's how I put it all together:

GLOVES. Some people might think gloves are either old-fashioned or high society. But nothing feels quite like slipping your hands into a pair of shiny, black patent leather or vinyl gloves. It makes me feel fancy and cool, like a rock 'n' roll lady (which is exactly what I am). The gloves make enough of a statement. I don't feel the need to put on a massive cocktail ring or a glitzy bracelet over a glove. That would be overkill.

SUNGLASSES. Movie-star shades are the way to go. I want them so big they take up half of my face, like my nose is going to crumble under the weight. I like black, but tortoiseshell is less severe, considering my black hair. My eyes are a lighter shade of brown, so when I pull down my shades and show my eyes, they're set off nicely by lighter-color frames.

SHOES AND BOOTS. What's on my feet is the most important part of any outfit. If I've got on nice boots or even a cool pair of heels, I feel like I could take over the world. Sandals, flats, stilettos, platform heels, pumps, I love them all (except wedges; can't say why exactly, I just don't like the look). Tall girls—like me, at five feet ten inches—should absolutely wear heels. This way, when there's a fight at the bar, you can see what's going on over everyone's head and find a clear path out of there.

I often start with the shoes and then build the rest of the outfit from the bottom up. Recently, I found a pair of chunky platform heels at the mall. They were color-blocked with white, yellow, orange, and teal. I knew I had to have them, even though I didn't know what to wear them with. And then, I was walking through Neiman Marcus and found a pair of palazzo pants in the same exact color palette. When I say exact, I mean it. You know how some musicians have perfect pitch? They can hear a note and know exactly what it is, F-sharp or B-flat or whatever? I have perfect color pitch. If I see a hue on a fabric swatch, I can recognize its perfect match in a dress. It's a gift.

Since I had the shoes, I bought the pants. I wore them with a yellow T-shirt from Marshalls to a spring charity event. Everyone else was wearing little black dresses. There I was, standing out in yellow, teal, orange, and white. Photographers went nuts and swarmed to take my picture. I felt like a million bucks. And it all started with the shoes.

JEANS. A nice-fitting pair gives you a look that says, "Don't fuck with me, I know what I'm doing." I wear jeans with everything. Paired with a fur coat, bling, and boots, you can go anywhere. Leather jeans—the best. I could be buried in mine, along with my diamonds.

LEATHER AND FUR. I love animals *and* animal skins. I don't see why I can't love both. I know some people are sensitive about this. My friend Jenn's daughter is a vegetarian, and she saw me wearing a vintage fox stole with the head still attached. She ran out of the room crying. In the case of an antique fur coat or a vintage leather jacket, that animal died a long, long time ago. The clothes already exist, so why not wear them?

Fur is the essence of luxury. A man who gives me a fur coat is a class act. It doesn't have to be the most expensive chinchilla. I just love the feel of mink or Mongolian lamb or angora—and I adore how it looks on me. When I put on my pink mink coat, black leather jeans, and leather, stiletto-heeled boots, I am one badass lady.

My basement is my fur storage. I've got a dozen coats down there. On heavy rotation lately: my colored fur coats. They are my signatures. I feel like a million bucks when I wear them. I also have a black-leather-and-zebra-print fur jacket that makes me feel pretty and tough. I wore it on *Jimmy Kimmel* and killed. I buy jackets that fit my shoulders and nip my waist. I can't button them because of my tits, so I just leave them open to show my cleavage and the shirt underneath.

66 A friend and I went to meet Ang at her time-share in Puerto Rico. We found her down on the beach. We could have spotted her from a mile away. She was wearing a canary-yellow bikini, with a dark tan and braids in her hair. She saw us and came running out of the water toward us, with the braids swinging like in the movie *Ten*, waving her arms and screaming, 'Hi, baby!' You could hear people all over the beach saying, 'Who the fuck is that?' Every single person, man or woman, was staring at her, just saying, 'Wow!' "

—*Angelina, friend*

PRINTS. Any animal print is a winner. Zebra. Leopard. Tiger. Cheetah. As soon as I put it on, I feel wild. If I've had the worst day ever—say, I got fired, found out my boyfriend was cheating, got robbed, broke a nail, whatever—I could put on a leopard-print shirt or dress and feel better instantly.

COLOR. Black is nice. It's flattering and comfortable. But men don't want to kiss girls in black. They like color, and so do I. As I mentioned, I have perfect color pitch and love the fashion challenge of finding cool matches, from shoes to bags to dresses. Whenever I do wear black—which is flattering on all Italian women, with our dark skin and hair—I add color to the outfit with accessories, dyed fur, hoop earrings with rainbow charms, dramatic gold jewelry, or red pumps. I love colors that go well with my tan skin tone. Sand, coral, brown, purple, pink, red, they all go great with Italian skin.

STRETCH. Obviously, for tops, I need stretch fabrics. I'm not about to put on a boring button-down shirt, so this isn't a real big style problem. Knit or cotton jersey accommodates me. If a top stretches across my boobs but tugs in my shoulders, I have to decide if the look is worth the discomfort. If it is, I say, "Fuck pain," and buy it.

SHINE. At least one thing on my body has got to reflect light. My nails and glossy lips add shine. But I like some of that sparkle in the outfit, too. It could be a fabric that shines, like satin or metallic sheen. It could be embellishments like beading or sequins. Or BLING (see below).

LABELS. I don't give a pickled rat's ass about labels. If the clothes look good on me and make me smile, I buy them. I don't have favorite designers, or any kind of brand loyalty. I don't look up at couture clothes or look down at mass retailers. I love what I love, at any price point, from any store or designer.

BLING IT ON!

Diamonds, diamonds, diamonds. (Or, when you're less flush, rhinestones, rhinestones, rhinestones.) I want to wear them all over, and I don't leave the house unless I'm dripping in bling. My diamond-stud nose piercing is my new favorite accessory. It's always there, and it's cool. How many grandmas out there have a diamond nose stud?

With earrings especially, the bigger, the better. Large hoops with sparkly charms look sexy and exotic with long, blown-out hair. But if I'm rocking high-drama earrings, I don't wear a necklace. If you're loaded down with earrings, *and* a necklace, *and* a meatball-size cocktail ring, *and* bangles, you might as well be wearing a sign that says, "Mug me in the parking lot."

> 66 One of her exes once bought Ang a ruby ring—eleven carats, with diamonds on either side. It was a stunner. She decided to turn the diamonds into rings for her and Raquel, and she had the ruby reset. A so-called friend came by the house and went into her bedroom, allegedly to see how it was decorated. He came out and left the house soon after. Ang went into her room that night, and instinct led her to check the jewelry box. The ruby ring was gone. She never went after the thief. Ang hates confrontation so much, she'd let some jerk walk away with her favorite piece of jewelry."
>
> —Little Ang, friend

DON'T BE A CLOTHES MISER

Say you find something nice in a store. You buy it, wear it out, and a friend or acquaintance asks where you got it. I know a lot of women who will lie about the store or say they bought it years ago, just to make sure the friend doesn't run out the next day and pick the item up for herself. Well, I'm not the type to keep a fashion find to myself. If I'm shopping (chances are, I either am or will soon be) and see something I know will look great on me *and* on a friend, I buy it in her size, too. So what if we have the same great stuff? What, so we might wind up wearing it to the same party? Oh, please. Get over it! That's hardly an epic tragedy. It's the opposite; it's funny! We play it up, stand next to each other, and strike the same pose. If anyone asks, we say, "We're two-for-one tonight."

"" When Big Ang goes shopping for herself, she winds up buying things for five other people, too. She could dress me with her eyes closed. Whether she went to Neiman Marcus or a vintage store, whatever she picks would fit me perfect and look great—and it'd be something I'd never pick out for myself. I always tell her, 'You should be an interior designer or a stylist.' But she'd rather work at the bar."

—Little Jenn, friend

DUMP THE DON'TS

I might fall in love with something in the store and spend a ton of money on it. But then, when I get it home, or wear it the first time, I realize I hate it. I've spent thousands on stuff that I wind up taking back. Any piece of clothing that lets me down—just like a man who disappoints me—has got to go. I show no mercy. I return it and buy something else. Or I give it away to a friend or donate it to Goodwill. Just because something doesn't work for me does not mean it's going to be a losah for someone else. But to work for me, it's got to be just right. A bad item of clothing can wreck an otherwise good night. Do not underestimate the potential horror of uncomfortable shoes.

" My friend took me and Ang to Philippe Chow's on East Sixtieth between Madison and Park. She was wearing these eight-hundred-dollar Gucci high-heeled shoes that matched her purse. She had a bad toe, and the shoes were killing her. To dull the pain, we started drinking Irish Car Bombs—Guinness with Jameson and Baileys—and barely ate the food. We wound up having it put in containers to go. My poor friend got stuck with a $1,100 bill, and no one ate the dinner! Ang was wacked on the Car Bombs, and when she got up, she started yelling about her 'scumbag shoes!' She took them off and walked around the restaurant, and then out on the street, in bare feet. When we got home, her feet were filthy and she had a bunch of little cuts on them. And the bad toe was a mess. We returned the scumbag shoes the next day."

—Neil, husband

ALWAYS KEEP 'EM GUESSING

My style doesn't get stale. When I've established a signature look, I don't just coast on it, because that's the best time to change it. The kiss of death with fashion is predictability. You could be wearing the loudest, hottest outfit ever, but if your friends have seen it fifteen times, you might get a yawn.

The best and only way to keep a wardrobe fresh: shopping. I shop a lot, online and in stores. The shopgirls at the Short Hills Mall in New Jersey (my favorite place to air out the credit card) all know me and love me. When they see me coming, they jump up and down for joy. I don't just shop at designer boutiques. One way to keep 'em guessing is to mix a pair of $20 sandals from DSW with a $2,000 designer dress and an old jean jacket you've had since forever. People look at me and say, "What the hell is she wearing?" But that's the point: they look.

Even when I was flat broke, I knew the value of keep-'em-guessing style. After my arrest by the Feds, I always looked my best for court and at the police station. One agent said that they couldn't wait for me to show up each morning to see what crazy outfit I would be wearing. I'm not saying that's why I got off with probation and house arrest, but I'm sure it didn't hurt.

5

Big House Rules

I've been moving every couple of years since birth. When I was growing up, we never stayed in one house longer than two or three years. We had five different places all over Brooklyn. I don't know exactly why my parents kept moving. Maybe it was because we needed bigger places to accommodate all those kids. As much as they argued—and they did, constantly—Mom and Dad did get along well in one particular way, producing seven kids in fifteen years. In order: Donna, Steven, Ronald, Louis, me, George, and Janine.

I moved out of my father's house for the first time at seventeen, and I've just kept moving ever since. If you spread out a map of New York City on the living room table and put in a pin on the location of my past addresses, your table would be destroyed. The trail covers parts of Brooklyn, Manhattan, and Staten Island. Since I had kids, we've moved fifteen times. I've lived in over twenty houses, and I'm planning another big move in a few weeks. My friend Jenn says, "Ang changes houses like other people change underwear."

As big a pain in the ass as moving is, I like it. If I stay in one place too long (I mean, a year or two), I get antsy and fantasize about some great new place that won't have any of the problems of the current location.

> **""** I hate moving constantly, but we're used to it."
>
> —*Raquel, daughter*

> **""** We've moved five times in five years. I'll never get used to it."
>
> —*Neil, husband*

IT'S JUST A FREAKIN' HOUSE

I've moved into beautiful beach houses and into run-down shitholes. No matter what condition the place is in when I get there, I fix it up according to my taste. Sometimes, I call Dominick, Janine's husband and my brother-in-law. He runs a construction company, and I have him renovate the bathrooms and the kitchen, knock out walls, the whole shebang. Next, I redecorate, which is the fun part, because of the shopping.

When the renovations and the new furniture are in place, I get to lie back on my couch and revel in how awesome it looks. Then, the itch to move or redecorate comes back. I find myself looking out the window as I drive around, wondering what it'd be like to live in this house, or that house. A lot of my moves have been only a few blocks apart. In New York, you can move less than a mile and it's like you've gone to a different universe—ideally, a ritzier one.

It's my nature to move. I'm always thinking about what's coming next, be it a house, a business, or a boyfriend. I don't fear change like a lot of people do. I rush toward the new and different. Even more than plastic surgery, a thirty-nine-year-old husband, a TV career, and always moving forward keep me young. Having a new project—like fixing up a house—keeps my creativity flowing and growing. The day that I lose interest in houses is the day I turn old. Not gonna happen.

I'm so looking forward to leaving the brick, Federal-style

house fans saw on *Mob Wives* season two, and into a fabulous new place nearby on Staten Island. It's got a huge kitchen and dining room, an in-ground pool, a Jacuzzi, a separate-entrance guesthouse (where Raquel and Sal will live; my husband is psyched about that), a bedroom for A.J., a twelve-car driveway with a three-car garage, built-in TVs, and surround sound. I'm just starting to pick out new furniture, which is exciting. I can already picture the parties I'm going to have, and the meals I'm going to cook there.

After twenty-one moves, though, house twenty-two is the last. I'm done. I'm tired. My kids are sick of it. Without a doubt, it's the best house yet. I can't improve on this. (Unless . . . no! Do not think about it!)

DON'T BE A CHEAP BASTARD

A cheapo asshole, like my old landlord, would rather let his own house crumble to the ground than spend a buck to maintain it. If one part of the fence is broken, he doesn't replace it. No, he lets it fall over and break the rest of the fence, too. Then he just leaves it there to rot! This is why I can't wait to leave this place and start fresh at a new house.

With houses and yards and pools, being cheap is just plain stupid. I spend as much as I can afford (or more than

I can afford) on repairs, so I won't be plagued by problems later. Like the air conditioner that falls out of the window into the driveway. Or a sink faucet that explodes and floods the kitchen. In the long run, it costs more to be cheap than it does to put up and shut up.

> " Angela could take a broken-down shack and make it look like the Plaza Hotel. For example, take the house she lives in now. When I first saw the shape it was in, I cried. Three years later, it's stunning. She's famous for taking a busted house, fixing it up, and flipping it. She's just as good as a garbage picker. She takes things that no one needs, works them over, and turns them into something everyone wants."
>
> —Little Jenn, friend

SAY YES TO DRAMA

You don't put a satin, leopard-print minidress on the queen. You don't put a beanbag chair and shag carpeting in a mansion. That's why, with each move, I decorate from scratch.

The Federal house on Little Clove Road, for example, I decorated with citrus colors: tangerine, lime, and purple. I threw in a life-size zebra statue and a leopard-print chair, a tangerine couch, a white globe chandelier over the glass dining room table, leopard-print-cushioned chairs, and purple shag carpeting. The whole flavor is fun, fresh, bright, light, a great place for Sal to play.

My new place is more sophisticated, and I'm thinking metallics, dark wood, and bigger pieces. I'm just starting to shop and conceptualize. I'm definitely going to paint the zebra black and call it a stallion.

I decorated Janine's place, the one Drita described as the "*Scarface* house" on *Mob Wives*. Dom built it, and it won a design award. It's got a three-story staircase right when you walk in. The rooms are all big and bright. The vibe of the house is epic, rich, and powerful. So that's how I decorated it. I thought color, texture, drama (decorating is when you can say yes to drama). Dark wood flooring and paneling, damask wallpaper, crown molding, crystal chandeliers, gold-framed oil paintings. Art everywhere. I go for surprising, tiny details, like brass-monkey toilet-paper holders, and intricate diamond-pattern inlays in the dining room table. I'm a pro at mixing patterns on upholstery. A chair could have a floral-patterned back and an animal-print seat. The kitchen has terra-cotta tiles and copper fixtures, all warm, sun-baked tones. It could be taken right out of a mansion in Tuscany. Wherever the eye goes, it'll find something interesting, beautiful, and fun. It's an amazing house. What you can see on *Mob Wives* is only a tiny portion of it.

KEEP IT IN THE FAMILY

Before I upgrade to a new place, I ask around. Who needs a kitchen table? Who wants chairs? Recycling is a great way to keep possessions in the family, and to help the younger generation fill their houses with old (but still cool) stuff.

DECORATE THE DRIVEWAY, TOO

Mint is one of my favorite words. It means the best, the coolest, the sharpest. To me, the ultimate mint car is a Jaguar. I've been through a dozen of them over the years. Some were gifts from boyfriends, like the convertible that I had a few years ago. But that wasn't practical with a grandson. Now I decorate my driveway with an XJ8 sedan. It's fully loaded, with Bluetooth, GPS—any option you can get, I got, and then some, including a lighted vanity mirror I use to put on lip gloss while doing seventy on the highway, which is a terrible habit I have to break. Hey, like I tell my kids, "Do as I say, not as I do."

> 66 Ang's first car? When she was seventeen, she showed up
> at the house with an Alfa Romeo Spider convertible with
> a stick shift. It looked great, but Ang didn't know how to
> drive it! She couldn't get it in first or second gear. She had
> to get the dealer to drive the car home for her. It was a
> classic case of Ang getting something she wants with the
> intention of figuring it out later."
>
> —*Janine, sister*

WHEN YOU STOP MOVING FORWARD, YOU DIE

My trend is upward. Every house is an improvement on the last. So, in that regard, I'm moving in the right direction. But the size of the place isn't the most important factor. Neither is the decorating. The greater happiness of any house comes from the people who live there, the joy they find in that place, and with each other.

THE DOOR IS ALWAYS OPEN

Wednesday afternoon. I'm sitting at the kitchen table with a bottle of wine. The front door is swinging open and closed, people wandering through, telling me their news, and having a quick bite to eat. They leave. Then a few more people cycle in, sit, talk, and eat. The sink fills up with plates and glasses, the ashtray gets emptied a few times. The day goes by, and I know I've been moving around busy the whole time, never bored, but I didn't really do anything. That's my life, every day. A house isn't a home unless it's full of people you love.

6
Big Travel Rules

When I travel, I do it in style. And I do love to get on a plane, dressed to the nines, and *go* somewhere. I hope no one gets mad at me for saying that the city of New York, amazing as it is, does not satisfy my every desire. Coney Island has a fine beach, but it doesn't compare to the Caribbean. Along with my urge to move houses, I have a real wanderlust. My first inclination is to go toward the sun and heat. In hot locales, I get to work on my tan, wear bikinis, and sip umbrella drinks.

❝ Years ago, we rented a Winnebago and drove to Florida to take the kids to Disney. It was nine kids, me, Janine, Ang, and another sister-in-law. We spent a week with their stepfather in Hollywood, Florida, and then a week in Orlando. We also stopped in Myrtle Beach. Ang got on a rented moped and was speeding around the place wearing a tube top with her Jamaican hair braids down to her ass. Those hicks got one look at her and almost crashed their cars into the guardrail. We were dying.

"Disney was great—exhausting, but fun. We decided to do the drive back to New York straight. I said, 'We're not stopping to eat until we get to Cracker Barrel.' Everyone said, 'Yeah, lunch at Cracker Barrel!' They all forgot that it was in North Carolina, like ten hours away. Of course, after a couple of hours, everyone wanted to stop, but I would not pull over.

"By the time we finally get there, we were all kind of punchy. We walked into the place and went into the gift shop. There was a huge display of stuffed animals, all elephants. I got behind the display and waited. Ang walked by, and I said, 'Hey, my name's Dumbo. What's yours?'

"She screamed, 'The elephants are talking!' She dragged over her sister-in-law and said, 'Listen to the elephant.'

"I said again, 'Hey, cutie. I'm Dumbo. What's your name?'

"Ang screamed again—'He's fucking talking to me! This thing is possessed!'—and ran out of there.

"Ten hours in a Winnebago with nine kids can do scary things to your mind."

—Dominick, brother-in-law

SECURE THE VALUABLES

I do tend to get ripped off on vacations. Once, when we went to Florida, our luggage was stolen right out of the car. I've left my purse on the beach while I've gone swimming and been ripped off. I have good luck in gambling and betting on horses. But bad luck with getting robbed. In the future, if I take jewelry with me, I'm going to wear every piece of it instead of leaving it in the room and never keep cash on me. If I get thirsty and want a drink? Well, I'll just wait for someone to buy me one. Should take, oh, about thirty seconds.

   ❝ A bunch of us took a trip to Aruba. Our hotel room was broken into. The door was literally off its hinges from being busted open. The management said we staged it and then tried to make us pay to repair the damage done by the thieves. That didn't go over well. When the security guard came to give us the bill, we took him hostage and tied him to a chair. Within the hour, we were kicked off the island and escorted to the airport by Aruba police."

—*Margo, friend and*
bartender at the Drunken Monkey

WHEN DRINKING ON PLANES, KEEP YOUR SEAT BELT ON AND SECURELY FASTENED

I'll let Jenn tell this one:

❝ We've taken a lot of trips together, Ang and our crew, and had many memorable moments. Like when we were on the plane to Puerto Rico, and Ang started saying, confusingly, that she had to get to her car. She goes to the plane's emergency door—we were thirty thousand feet in the air—thinking that's the exit door of the club. (No shocker: she'd had a bit too much to drink.) The other passengers were freaking out. We got her to sit down. When we landed, she said, 'Are we home yet?' This was before 9/11, obviously. If it'd happened after, she probably would have been put in a Puerto Rican prison.

"On another trip, Andrew Dice Clay was on our flight to the Bahamas. One look, and he fell instantly in love with Ang and invited her to smoke a joint in the airplane bathroom. I don't know what went on in there, but when we landed, Dice followed her all over the island."

—*Little Jenn, friend*

IT'S NOT ABOUT WHERE YOU GO, BUT WHO YOU GO WITH

First rule of travel: take your crew with you. Friends, kids, whoever wants to come should. I never left my daughter and son behind when I took a vacation. Why do that? They're fun to have around, and we get to spend time together outside the day-to-day existence at home. This is one of the reasons we're all so close. My kids know I enjoy having them around.

Even my honeymoon in Long Branch, New Jersey, was a group trip. My sister and her family, my own kids, Sal, and the rest of my crew stayed in a big house on the beach. Neil might've expected we'd go on a romantic getaway. Ha! I'm not the romantic type. Now he knows, if he didn't when we got married.

One memorable family trip we took was a cruise to Hawaii. Raquel got so seasick, we had to leave the boat and find a hotel. Turned out, we had to pay a penalty to get off the ship and rearrange our airfare. A $15,000 cruise wound up costing $50,000. Which was, of course, *horrible*. But Hawaii was the best. Once Raquel stopped throwing up, we had a nice time.

7

Big Going Out
Rules

The movie *Saturday Night Fever* could have been filmed at Pastels, the legendary disco in Brooklyn that I used to go to back in the day. When I was dancing on the tables there in the eighties, every guy looked like Tony Manero. Wiseguys held court in the VIP room where Margo worked and made the club their official headquarters. And I was there for all of it. Bars and clubs are where I grew up. They're where I've earned a living, met my friends, husbands, boyfriends. What can I say? I love the nightlife.

66 Mom once coat-checked me when I was a baby. I was asleep in my car seat, and she parked me at the coat check. I stayed there and slept for hours under the coats. Mom gave the girl a nice tip."

—*Raquel, daughter*

FIRST TO COME, LAST TO LEAVE

Fashionably late? What's the point? You miss out on an hour of partying. When my crew and I go to a club, we get there for happy hour, and we close the place. We're still sitting at the bar when the cleaning staff shows up at dawn. The way we roll at the clubs: we don't pay to get in, and we're never told to go. You know how you might be talking to a friend the day after a big night out, and she tells you about some sick shit that went down after you left? That never happens to me because I'm the last to go. And if some sick shit went down, I'm usually at the center of the action anyway.

AS LONG AS THE FOOD IS GOOD, I'M THERE

I go out for dinner probably four nights a week. It's fun from beginning to end: figuring out where we want to go, getting dressed, walking into a restaurant and seeing five friends at the bar, ordering a cocktail before dinner, and then settling in at a table loaded down with plates and glasses that I won't have to wash later (my nails can only take so much scrubbing). I gravitate naturally to people who love food as much as I do. Some of my best friends own world-class restaurants within a few miles of my house in Staten Island, which is convenient for me.

My friend Angelina (another Ang, but she's not an Angela) has a place, Angelina's Ristorante, which is a freestanding Victorian house. It has seating on three levels—including in the backyard—right on the water. Every one of her dishes makes my mouth water, but if I had to recommend a couple of things above all else, I'd say the pasta with Bolognese sauce and her veal chop.

Walking into Bella Mama Rose, owned by my friend John, is like a scene from *This Is Your Life*. On any given night, I might run into a neighbor or a childhood friend or the mother of an ex. Of course, I stop and say hello to everyone. Just getting through the room to sit down at a table can take half an hour. The food is To. Die. For. Ravioli in cream sauce.

Pasta, lobster, antipasti. I'm not going to read you the whole menu, but you can't go wrong with anything on it. And the portions are enormous. If you order a "family style" serving, you could feed the block . . . all of them are probably family anyway.

Restaurants run in the family, too. My brother-in-law Dom's sandwich shop, the Square, on Forest Avenue in Staten Island, makes the juiciest roast beef and (homemade) mozzarella sandwich in New York. A.J. is the manager at Ignazio's in Brooklyn, right under the Brooklyn Bridge. They make the best pizza in the borough, and A.J. is doing great there. So proud of my boy!

" Ang bartended at my parents' house for their New Year's Eve parties. I was drawn to her immediately. I'm ten years younger than Ang and Celia, but I started going to clubs with them. She'd march into Pastels and announce, 'I'm going to the VIP section.' She just knew where to go, who to talk to, what to wear, what to drink. I was in awe. She always looked out for me, like an aunt. And she corrupted me in a good way—with bad boys."

—Renee, Mob Wives castmate

LET THE WISEGUYS PAY

When I go to a mob hangout to eat or drink, nine times out of ten, someone will pick up the bill. It's not about hitting on me. I could be there with my grandson and daughter. I could be with my husband, or a dozen friends. When the meal is over and I call for the check, I'm just told that it's been taken care of. Sometimes, I go out, and a plate of food or a round of drinks is sent over to our table, and some wiseguy I haven't seen in twenty years raises his glass to me. Or I go out to eat with ten people, we order bottles of wine, Caesar salad, pasta, lobsters, tiramisu, and then the bill comes and it's $100. I ask, "How can ten people stuff themselves with lobster for ten bucks apiece?" The restaurant owner says, "It's taken care of." Why does this happen? It's courtesy and loyalty. If a wiseguy sees an old friend—someone who's always been kind to him and laughed with him and kept her mouth shut—he buys her dinner.

And now, with being on TV, forget it!

TIP BIG

I make up for the free food by leaving generous tips. I walk around with a stack of bills and dole them out to each person who works there. I know from working in bars and clubs that every single person in the operation deserves some credit. Fifteen or 20 percent for the waiter doesn't cover what goes into getting food on the table. Since the waiters give part of their tips to the kitchen crew, I tip 30 percent, 40 percent. I spend more on tips than I do on alcohol. The bathroom girl gets a twenty. The valet gets a twenty. And the bartender—well, I have a special fondness for all bartenders—gets five bucks per beverage. You want to know how to go straight to heaven? Tip often and tip big.

❝ Most of the time, Ang doesn't have to pay when she goes out. On the rare occasions when the bill does come, and it's a big group, Ang's rule is to split the bill evenly. Even if you had only drinks and everyone else is ordering food. Or if you have just an appetizer and everyone else is having entrées. You all have to chip in and pay equal amounts. It doesn't matter if you sat down and didn't order *anything* to eat or drink. If you're at the table, you share the bill.

"Now, a lot of people don't agree with it. They say, 'I'm not going to eat, so I shouldn't have to pay.' Big Ang doesn't care. She says, 'You didn't order anything, but you ate off everyone's plate!' I happen to agree with Ang. It's about being fair. One night, maybe you do just pick at other people's plates. The next night, you might order more than anyone else. When you're talking about hundreds of dinners over a lifelong friendship—and all of Ang's friends have been in her life forever—it evens out in the end."

—Celia, friend

BETTER TO BE LOOKED OVER THAN OVERLOOKED

I love dressing up to go out and feeling like a million bucks. When I glide into a club in a choice outfit, I know everyone there will turn around to look at me and think, "Who the hell is that?" Love me or hate me, they will look.

Like that old saying, when you walk into a room, the best reaction is that everyone cheers. The second-best reaction: everyone boos. But the worst reaction is that no one even realizes you're there. Dress to make an impression. Otherwise, you might as well have stayed home.

66 I've known Ang since the eighties, and whenever she walked into a bar, she was always a head turner, always happy, always beautifully dressed. One night, I was working after hours at a bar in Brooklyn, and Ang walked in at 4:00 a.m. The entire place turned to look at her. She was drenched, head to toe, like a drowned rat, and her dress was so short it was higher than her underwear, like a go-go dress from the sixties. Even for her, that was *short*. I asked, 'Uh, you went out like that?'

"She said, 'I was on a dinner cruise and it rained the whole time. Only I could go on a cruise and get soaked for four hours!'

"The dress, at the start of the night, was a normal length. But as it dried, on her drive over to the bar, it shrank right on her body. It was like a doll dress now! But she didn't care. She told the story, and everyone there was cracking up. She sat down at the bar and had a drink."

—Denise, friend

❝ My first date with Ang, we went to Bay Ridge, Brooklyn, to a steak house with a long line out front. Ang skipped the line and went right into the restaurant. The maître d' greeted her like visiting royalty (she *is* the Queen of Bay Ridge, I came to learn). He gave us a table immediately— no reservations. The best table in the house. The waiters started bringing us food right away. It was crazy, like a scene from *GoodFellas*. I'd never experienced anything like it before.

"Then Ang wanted to go to a club, so we went to a place called Suite. I guess it used to be a famous disco, Pastels, and Ang had been going there since she was a kid. I'd never been there before, but I was amazed. It was a huge guido club. The line of people waiting to get in was around the corner. Ang was driving a two-seater convertible at the time. She pulled up, got out of the car, and left it running in the middle of the street with the door open. I asked if that was okay, and she said, 'It's fine. Come on.' We walked toward the club entrance. It took forever because Ang knew like everyone on the line to get in, and they all wanted to say hello. When we got to the front, the bouncer ran over to her to let her right in. There was a bachelorette party on line waiting to get in, and Ang said, 'They're with me, too,' and the bouncer let them all in.

"We went back to the VIP section and drank all night. But we never got asked for money. There was no bill, at the restaurant or the club. Even before she was on TV, everyone knew her. She was treated like a celebrity before she was one. I said to myself, 'What the hell have I gotten myself into?'

"Now I know. Every day with Ang is an adventure."

—Neil, husband

ON THE WAY HOME, WATCH OUT FOR COPS

There is such a thing as calling too much attention to yourself—like when you catch the eye of a cop. I'll let Dom tell the stories.

" Ang was driving across the Verrazano Bridge at seven a.m. one morning after being up all night. She was speeding. Cops pulled her over on the side of the highway. As soon as they saw Ang, they had her get out of the car. They said, 'We'll let you go if you hop up and down on one foot and sing 'Raindrops Keep Fallin' on My Head.' So she did it, and the cops sent her on her way. There're some advantages to having big boobs."

—Dominick, brother-in-law

" Back in 1993, I bought a used minivan. Ang took it to go to Joe's Clam Bar in Sheepshead Bay to get dinner. An hour and a half later, the cops called and said they had Ang for driving a stolen car. I go down to the precinct and see Ang in the cage. I said, 'It's my van. I'll switch places with her.'

"Ang said, 'No way! My sister will kill me if you lock up her husband!'

"I insisted and took her place. It turned out to be a tag job. The previous owners switched the ID numbers from another van onto the one I bought. When the cops went to the guy I bought the van from, he was gone. So I lost the van, but no charges were brought.

"The kicker to the story is, the original reason Ang got stopped in the first place wasn't because she was speeding. A cop saw her getting into the car, and he wanted to find out where she lived, maybe track her down and ask her out. He ran the number on the van and saw there was a problem. Then next thing you know, she's in the cage. So there are some disadvantages to having that body, too."

—*Dominick, brother-in-law*

JUST GO!

Get out of the house! Don't zone out in front of the TV, eating crappy food and sinking into the couch. Life is happening out in the world, and it's not so far away. You only have to go as far as the corner bar. Even if you just watch TV there, you'll be with other people. Being where the action is keeps you involved and in touch with friends, your neighbors, and the world. And that keeps you looking and feeling young. A drink at the local watering hole is a lot cheaper than a facelift! Think about it.

8

Big Lifestyle Rules

here style and life meet: the lifestyle. In our culture, when people say "the Lifestyle," they mean the Family. The Mob. The Mafia. Cosa Nostra. Martin Scorsese movies and *The Sopranos* are pretty accurate, as far as I've seen of the Lifestyle. It's exciting. The gifts and houses can't be beat. But it's also heartbreaking. When a loved one is sent to prison and dies behind bars, it's not so glamorous. At this point, the *GoodFellas* era is over. Everyone is in jail or dead. And the ones who are alive are informers. The old codes are forgotten, but the legend lives on.

KNOW YOUR HISTORY

If you are "connected," you are most likely blood-related to at least one person in a Family. The Five Families ruled "organized crime" in the New York/New Jersey area. In alphabetical order (*not* order of preference; I don't want to piss off anyone), they are the Bonanno, Colombo, Gambino, Genovese, and Lucchese families. They originated in the early twentieth century when Sicilian immigrants came to New York to make a better life for themselves. During the Great Depression, times were hard, and the Italian immigrants banded together. Because there wasn't a lot of work to be had, they took to the streets and committed crimes to feed their children. The leaders of the Cosa Nostra also protected their neighborhoods and made sure that outsiders weren't ripping off their own people.

I have connections to each of the Five Families, by blood, friendship, or romance. Just by living where I grew up in Brooklyn, you were exposed to the culture. I've dated guys from every crew. Celia's brother Anthony Graziano is a high-ranking member of the Bonanno family. My *Mob Wives* castmate Karen's father, as everyone knows, was the underboss of the Gambino family. My mother's brother Salvatore "Sally Dogs" Lombardi was a capo in the Genovese family. He spent twenty-two years in prison and died behind bars.

FLEX YOUR EMOTIONAL MUSCLES

The women in the Lifestyle have to stay strong. They're as strong as the men. We're out here, making a living, keeping the family going while the men are in jail. I'm not saying prison is easy. But it's tough to be on the outside, watching people you love get locked up, and having to wait for them to get out. Meanwhile, you have to hold in your feelings and pretend to be happy when you see them in court or in prison. The idea is to remind them what they have to look forward to when (if) they get out. It's the mob version of a game face.

66 If Angela is sad, you'll never know it. She's always happy, always the life of the party. She's seen enough sadness in her life. She doesn't want to see that when she looks in the mirror or affect anyone else if she is in a bad mood."

—Denise, friend

GET A NICKNAME

The tradition of nicknames goes way back to Charlie "Lucky" Luciano and Al "Scarface" Capone, and it lives on today. In January of 2011, the NYPD busted over a hundred wiseguys from all over the city. The list of nicknames on the indictments was like a *Who's Who of the Five Families* or the Mafia *Social Register*. Tony Bagels. Johnny Bananas. Junior Lollipops. Vinny Carwash. The Little Man. The Old Man. Mush. Gooch. The Claw. Cheeks. Fatty. Lumpy. Nighthawk.

The nickname comes from your personality or your physical appearance. In *GoodFellas*, Henry Hill explained how Jimmy Two Times got his handle: "He said everything twice, like, 'I'm gonna go get the papers, get the papers.'" My uncle Sal was kind of a mad dog, so he was called Sally Dogs. If you have oversize, yellow teeth, you might get tagged Johnny Horse. If you always wear pants that are too short, you might get stuck with Tommy Socks. In the old days, cops planted bugs all over the social clubs, in bars, cars, and houses. The wiseguys knew they couldn't talk privately on the phone or even in their homes and places of business. So, instead of doing a walk-and-talk outside, they substituted the real names with colorful, descriptive nicknames instead.

The nickname Big Ang has nothing to do with my boobs. It's due to my height—five feet ten inches in flats. I got it when I was twelve, hanging around with my friend Angela, who was small. She was Little Ang, and I got tagged Big Ang. (Angela is a common name in my culture. In just our family, there are five Angelas or Angelinas. If you yelled "Hey, Ang!" into the crowd at the San Gennaro festival in Little Italy, half the women on the street would turn around.)

> 66 Ang got the name because she was big and the other Angela was little. But the reason the nickname stuck has nothing to do with her boobs or lips or height. It's because of her big heart and her big personality."
>
> —Raquel, daughter

YOU CAN'T TAKE IT WITH YOU

My people are not big savers. Wiseguys like to see their money in action. They wear it, drive it, clasp it in diamond form around the necks of their wives, goomadas, and girlfriends. They invest it in real estate and business. If they do save cash, they don't put it in a bank, but under the floorboards in their kid's bedroom closet.

As soon as I get my hands on some money, I spend it. I spoil myself, my kids, and my friends with gifts. Hey, I'm not taking the money with me when I die. And I'm not putting it away in a bank until I'm too old to enjoy it.

The bar is a cash business, so I usually pay for things that way. Even jaded store owners' eyes get big when I slap down some hundreds on the counter. People warn me, "You're going to have nothing when you're older." But this advice has holes six feet deep. When I'm older, who cares if I've got nothing? I'll be old and decrepit and wouldn't be able to enjoy it anyway. But now, I'm still young enough to travel where I want, spoil my grandson, and look good in my clothes. I'm living as high a life as I can, for as long as I can. And that means spending, not saving. You can't take it with you. This habit only turns bad when I spend my money *before* I get my hands on it, which is too often.

BUSTING OUT HAPPENS

Rainy days do come. I have a handful of failed businesses behind me to attest to that. Nocturnals was the last one I had to put out of business, and it broke my heart. That place was the coolest. It was a local watering hole, like the Drunken Monkey, where people could come to unwind after a hard day, see friends, talk trash, throw a punch, get stabbed. You know, a typical neighborhood bar. Drita from *Mob Wives* used to go there with her friends when she was a kid. She got in fights every night. It was crazy. But no matter how high tempers flared, or how many drinks people had, no one would ever rat you out, even if the cops showed up. If the bouncer got stabbed, he'd just go to the hospital and tell them he tripped onto a blade. Four times.

Jenn and I ran a kid's party place, like a Chuck E. Cheese, called Imagination for a while. She'd be out front doing the chicken dance with the kids, and I'd be in back making grilled-cheese sandwiches. That place lasted about a year before we closed down.

When the money stops flowing in, I hock my jewelry. I put a FOR SALE sign in front of my house and in the windshield of my car. (People have asked me, "You were given all this stuff by your boyfriends. What happened to it?" Well, now you know—sold or stolen.) And then I go out there and get a new job. That's what I've noticed about life: No matter how rainy it gets—and it could be like Hurricane Irene for years—eventually, the sun comes back out.

And when it does, I go shopping.

66 It's all about instant gratification for Ang. If she wants to get Neil a car, she goes out and buys a car. She wants to go eat? We go. I was with her when she got her first check from the TV show, and we immediately went to the most

expensive store in SoHo. She bought two thousand dollars' worth of shoes for each of us. But it doesn't matter if Ang has a dollar in her pocket or a thousand, she looks like a million bucks. It doesn't matter if it's bologna or filet mignon, she eats well. Ang will share whatever she's got. If she's got nothing, she'll borrow it—and she always pays you back."

—*Little Jenn, friend*

❝ We've all been impressed by Ang's resilience. No matter what happens, she picks herself up and starts over without complaining. I don't know where it comes from exactly. She had a tough childhood and had to take care of herself very young. I think it's her natural personality. She has a positive outlook on life, and things just roll off her back."

—*Rita, aunt*

MAKE THE CALL

Growing up, I couldn't throw names around like Mafia princesses do. But I did make a few calls in my day. When I was eighteen and had just broken up with my first husband, I saw him at a bar I liked. He acted like an asshole and gave me a hard time. I got so pissed, I picked up a tray of empty glasses and threw it at him. (FYI, my "no fighting" rule has one exception: ex-husbands.) Anyway, we couldn't both stay at this bar, and he refused to leave. I wasn't about to be chased out of one of my favorite places. So, I picked up the phone and called Uncle Sally. I explained the situation. The next thing I know, my ex is being dragged out of the bar, and word came down that if I ever showed up, he had to leave immediately. Just to mess with him, I went there every single night for months and watched him run out the door in terror. Never got old.

DON'T BE A RAT

Omertà is how I live. I don't rat. Never have. Never gonna. In this Lifestyle, the values are (1) love and respect your family, (2) don't rat, and (3) take your secrets to the grave. I'm serious about this. I can talk about a lot of stuff, but you will never hear certain stories from me about the old days. Those will be buried with me (along with my leather jeans and diamonds).

That's not working out for a lot of other people, obviously. Hardly anyone sticks with the code of silence anymore. Everyone is a rat. The number one mob term you hear on the street these days isn't "take it to the mattresses" or "sleep with the fishes." Instead, you hear "informer" and "cooperating with the Feds." When I was arrested and my feet were put to the fire, I didn't rat. It wasn't that hard not to betray my friends. I just sat there and didn't say a word.

If you inform, you can expect to lose every friend you had. Go in the witness protection program, you might as well be dead. As the saying goes, you make your bed, you die in it.

ASK ME NO QUESTIONS . . .

. . . and I'll tell you no lies. Any barrage of questions feels like the third degree. When a boyfriend asks, "Where you been?" I instantly resent him for wondering. If I wanted him to know where I was or what I was doing, he would. Nosing around in my business makes me feel like my privacy is being violated, which is bad enough. But when someone starts asking me a certain type of question—like, "So, did you hear what went down last weekend?" or "What's up with this or that situation?"—I get suspicious. My guard goes up. Ask me too many questions, the conversation is ovah.

> "I guess some people didn't like the very idea of a show about the Lifestyle called *Mob Wives*. As a mob daughter, I couldn't do it. My dad would turn over in his grave. But he would be on Ang's side. He'd support her decision. He loved Ang to death. When she came to visit my dad in prison, we had the best times. He was there for twenty-two years. We used to smuggle in liquor, and Viagra for visits with my mother. When we'd show up, it made his day. If he could see what's happening for Ang, he'd be overjoyed. We all are!"
>
> —Sallyann, cousin

PAY YOUR RESPECTS

Why does it always seem like someone from the old neighborhood, or a friend from way back, is dropping dead? Because they are! If someone I know dies, I go to the funeral. Period. I have to. It's how I pay my respects to the deceased, and the family. For people I was close to, I do the whole day—funeral, burial, and a visit to their house later. For an acquaintance or casual friend, I just run in for two minutes, long enough to show my face and say, "Sorry for your loss," kiss-kiss, and wave good-bye. Sometimes, I go to the funeral parlor expecting to stay for ten minutes and wind up staying for an hour.

Raquel thinks I'm OCD about going to Every. Single. Funeral. She calls me a "coffin chaser." Going to so many funerals is a major undertaking (no pun intended). But I have a reputation for showing up to funerals. So now if I *don't* go, it's an insult.

I can't bring food and flowers or I'd go broke. And I don't even wear black. These days, it's passé to wear black to funerals. A lot of people show up in tracksuits. I go in whatever I'm already wearing. No one gives a crap. They're just happy to see me. In our world, where family and loyalty mean everything, it matters how many people come to a funeral. It is a measure of how well respected and loved the person was.

I have to admit, when I go to funerals, I do think about the fact that, one day, I'll be the one lying down in satin at the front of the room. And when I do? I want to be laid out at the site of the old Pastels, and not in a funeral parlor. And that room? It'd better be freakin' packed! I'll be watching from beyond!

GO THE DISTANCE

Last week, I went with Celia to visit my "uncle" in prison. He's really Celia's uncle, but I've known him forever. We drove the hour and a half to Sing Sing in Ossining, New York, on a Monday morning. Sing Sing is a maximum-security prison, so the rules for visiting are seriously strict. They have a schedule for when visitors can come in, and they count off a certain number at a time. If you miss the count, you have to wait for two hours. When you're allowed inside, the visitors go to a waiting room. The guards take all of the names, put them in a hat, and pull one for a random drug test. Go figure: they picked me. It's always me. I'm constantly being asked to pee into a cup. (I passed the test, thank you very much.)

I made the mistake of wearing a bra with a metal clasp on the back. It was just a quarter-inch thin wire, but it didn't matter. I set off the metal detector. I had to go into a bathroom (where you can't run the water or flush the toilet, or they'll think you're getting rid of something), remove the bra, put it in a bag to be examined, walk back through the metal detector, go to a *different* bathroom, and put the bra back on. You can't go back to the same bathroom because you might've stashed something in there before.

This visit, not only did I have to do the drug test and go on tour of the prison restrooms, but the guards made me put on a white chef coat over my top. They said the V-neck T-shirt I had on showed too much cleavage (only a couple of inches, which, for me, is like a nun's habit). Apparently, if the prisoners saw my chest, they'd go crazy. This whole process of waiting for the count, taking the drug test, getting through the checkpoints, and everything took three hours. We were standing up the whole time. Fortunately, I wore sneakers.

We finally got to sit at a table with my "uncle." We hung out and talked with him about what's going on. When you visit someone in prison, you have to keep it light. You're there to cheer the guy up, not complain or dump your problems on him. The idea is to give him some company and a break in the routine.

I always bring a big stack of singles with me. The visiting room has dozens of vending machines with all kinds of food that the prisoners don't get to eat day to day. Back when I used to visit Uncle Sally, I'd bring $200 in change and he'd eat everything in the place. White Castle, KFC, candy bars, he'd clean the machines out. In the old days, it was easier to smuggle in food for the inmates during visitation. My mom used to smuggle in vodka in baby bottles. I used to hide fully cooked lamb chops under my boobs. Once, I was surrounded by bugs in the prison yard because they could smell the veal cutlets I'd put in my bra.

The guards don't let you touch or kiss excessively, but we were allowed to take some pictures with our uncle. I hate the photo of me in that big white coat buttoned up to my neck. Next time, I'll remember not to wear anything too revealing. Don't want to risk riling up the inmates.

A FRIEND TODAY MIGHT BE AN ENEMY TOMORROW

I was arrested once. The circumstances that led up to it are why my guard goes up when people ask too many questions. I thought I could trust someone—I'll call her Scumbag—and she stabbed me in the back. Being ratted out feels like a violation. It's hard to trust anyone again. My guard has been up 24–7 since it happened to me.

The day of my arrest back in 2001, I was driving my car, and three or four cop cars suddenly surrounded me and blocked me in. They pulled me over into a secluded spot. I found out later why they did the roadside intercept. If they'd gone to my house, the word would go out that I'd been picked up. If no one knew about it, they could try to flip me. But they had no idea who they were talking to.

" I knew something was wrong. I was waiting for Ang and she didn't show up. Then I got a phone call. She said, 'Take care of my kids.' And that was it. I flew into a panic. No one knew what was going on, and then to get that scary call? I got her kids and we waited to hear from her again—but didn't for ten hours."

—Janine, sister

The cops drove me around all day. While I was in the car, they played the tapes that Scumbag had recorded of me. She'd worn a wire and followed me into the bathroom once. On the tapes, I could hear myself peeing. It was gross. I heard myself talking about my side job of selling pot and cocaine out of the bar I was working at the time, talking about the product quality, and the logistics of selling it and cash transfers. As I listened, I fell deeper and deeper into shock. Not only was I in deep shit, someone I had thought of as a friend had put me there.

The detectives drove me around the neighborhood and asked me about my friends, my business, hammering away all day to get me to talk. They had to stop for gas twice (but no food or bathroom breaks, pricks). They asked me about selling coke and about a couple of friends of mine who'd recently died. They asked if I knew who was responsible. The pressure was on. But the detectives couldn't flip me. I guess they figured, if we can't make her crack after ten hours, she probably won't, ever. They took me in and officially arrested me. The charge was possession of cocaine—I had fourteen bags of it on me when they picked me up—and selling drugs.

People ask me why I did it. I was a single mom, supporting my family, paying $3,000 in rent. I did it for the money. I wouldn't do it again and haven't since. I learned my lesson. It's not worth the risk. But the bigger lesson was to be careful who you let into your life. Scumbag is now in the witness protection program, and she can rot in hell for all I care.

DO THE TIME

Because of those tapes (and a lot of other evidence), fourteen people were arrested in what the DEA and NYPD called Operation White Heat. On the totem pole of those arrested, I was on the bottom rung. I was only in jail for one day. I put up a $100,000 bond and was sent home.

Two years later, I pleaded guilty to selling cocaine. I was sentenced to three years' probation and four months of house arrest. Of the other fourteen defendants in the sting, eight also got probation. Six went to prison. Some are still there.

During my house arrest, I had to wear a monitor so the Feds knew where I was at all times. I was living on Townsend Avenue then, right next door to Raquel's boyfriend's family. We were all good friends, so that helped. My girlfriends and family came by every day. That also made me feel less claustrophobic. But for someone like me who needs to be where the action is and loves to go out, being confined to one place was torture. The only way to get through it was to keep myself distracted and busy. Here're my suggestions if you do find yourself under house arrest:

1. **HIRE A TRAINER.** Mine came every week and made me sweat. Loved the trainer; hated the workouts. But they did help me burn off a lot of nervous energy and kept me from going batshit crazy.

2. **MARK THE EXPERIENCE.** Cari-Ann came over with her ink and needles once, and we had a little at-home tattoo party. She gave some of us new tats on our toes of ladybugs and cherries. Of course, we had to open a few bottles of Opus One to dull the pain.

3. **BRING THE PARTY TO YOU.** I should say "parties." We had a New Year's Eve party at my place, and everyone came with bottles of champagne and platters of food. I'm sure the Feds enjoyed watching us have a great time from their van down the block. We toasted the New Year, which would bring my freedom. We kept the party going until the next day, and the day after that. What else was I gonna do? Roll into a ball and cry?

4. **HAVE SLEEPOVERS.** It was like being back in junior high, inviting all the girls to come sleep over to drink, eat, and talk about boys.

5. **DRAW THE BLINDS.** I was so sick of staring at those four walls, I opened all the blinds and curtains. I'd walk

around in the house wearing whatever (or not wearing much of anything). It didn't occur to me that someone might be watching. My neighbor across the street had been tuning in to my front windows like a TV set. I was his personal reality TV show. I guess I might've been kind of entertaining in my daily fashion show (I tried on a lot of outfits to kill the time). So this psycho creep started putting love letters in my mailbox, along with little gifts. I had no idea who was sending them, and the letters freaked me out. But, since I was being watched by the Feds, too, a cop was always nearby. I wasn't scared the creep would do anything. I did draw the blinds, though.

6. **BUILD A STRONG FENCE.** The one time I violated my house arrest was totally by accident. We had a dog at the time, Joey. That poor dog was going stir-crazy, too. The kids took him on walks, and we put him out in the yard. But he wanted to run. Anyway, one day I open the front door to let someone in, and Joey nosed his way around my legs. He took off like a shot. I said, "Oh, shit," and ran after him. I was in the moment. I didn't think about what I was doing. But sure enough, the alarm went off, and the next thing I know, a cop car pulls up alongside me on the street as I'm running after the dog.

The cop said, "Where do you think you're going?" or something like that, as if I was going to make a break for it in my bathrobe and slippers.

"My dog ran away."

"Get in."

I did, and the cops drove me around until we found Joey. I appreciated the help. But I bet they wanted to find the dog just to make sure I wasn't bullshitting them about why I'd gone on the lam. For half a block.

WITHOUT HONOR, YOU'VE GOT SHIT

Wherever you are, whoever you're with, if you don't respect yourself, nothing else matters. That's what honor means to me, and I'll never give that up. I'd rather live in a Dumpster than sacrifice my integrity, rat out a friend, or betray a family member. Honor is my lifestyle, and it's the core of my relationships, too.

PART 2

RELATIONSHIPS

AS I SAID BEFORE, ONE OF THE TWO THINGS you can control in life is how you treat other people. My relationship philosophy is to always be kind, caring, and generous with my family and friends. I don't want to look back on my life and think, "I really let everyone down." I want to think, "I did right by my loved ones. And everyone loved me back."

9

Big Food Rules

Relationships and food go together like sausage and peppers. The main action of most relationships plays out in the kitchen or over the table. Family dinners. Romantic meals. Reunion barbecues. We Italians, especially, pour our hearts and souls into food. I do it because I'm cooking for the people I care about. You can literally taste the emotions that go into any meal I cook, whether it's pastini with butter for Sal each morning, meatballs for my husband, or fried chicken cutlets for my son.

Our days revolve around what and where we're going to eat for two reasons: (1) we're hungry! and (2) it's the next time we'll gather together. At breakfast, we're planning dinner. At dinner, we're planning breakfast. Food isn't just some crap to pick up at the drive-through. Eating is how we enjoy life, and cooking is a way to show our creativity and love.

SUNDAY IS SACRED

The Sunday dinner tradition goes back to my childhood. My mother, Jean, made a feast for our family every week—and there were a lot of us. Besides the seven kids, our friends, aunts, uncles, and cousins would always show up, too, and right on time to eat. They'd crawl out of the woodwork. It was like they stuck their noses in the air from halfway across Brooklyn and said, "Mmmm, smells like dinner's ready."

The first course was always pasta with gravy. We don't say *sauce*. We say *gravy*. Sauce is thin. Gravy is thick. When people say *sauce*, I think of tomato water. No, thank you. Sunday gravy has all kinds of braised meats in it—sausage, meatballs, spareribs, braciola. In my gravy, I throw in pig's knuckles and pigskin rolled with herbs, garlic, and cheese. (Hungry yet?) The base is Pastene tomatoes and wine. It simmers for hours. The smells in the house are beyond belief, incredible.

The second course was a roast—whatever looked good that week, be it pork or a fresh ham or beef. No heavy marinade or rub. My mom would just sprinkle the meat with garlic powder, salt, and pepper, put in the oven at a low temperature, and cook it all day until it was soft and juicy and full of flavor. With the roast, Mom would put out vegetables sautéed in olive oil, roast potatoes, or a potato pie, and a simple salad of iceberg lettuce, red onion, tomatoes, and cucumber dressed with vinaigrette. For dessert, we'd get cannolis or pastries from a local baker.

Then Sunday dinner extended into Monday breakfast with Italian French toast. We'd take slices of leftover Italian twist bread with sesame seeds on top, soak them in an egg batter with salt, pepper, and grated Romano cheese, then fry them in olive oil. Just try it one morning. You will never eat regular French toast again.

We have a special Sunday drink, too: red wine mixed with cream soda. After I made a glass of it for A.J. on an episode of *Mob Wives*, the drink blew up and now it's a bona fide thing. People are calling it the Big Ang.

So many of my memories of my mom are in the kitchen, standing at the stove, frying a stack of pork chops. Raquel and A.J. didn't get to know her, but they do know the stories about how Grandma Jean cooked Sunday dinner for the neighborhood. And now my sisters and I uphold the tradition. We don't stick to Mom's menu exactly, but the spirit is the same. Sunday is group cooking day. If you come by, be prepared to start frying. Or to chop vegetables, dredge cutlets, roll meatballs. The feast feeds anywhere from fifteen to twenty-five people, so everyone—including the kids—pitches in. We stand shoulder to shoulder in the kitchen doing prep work and manning the stove. Whoever's in town comes over for the meal—family, friends, their kids, their grandkids. If it seems like we're feeding everyone in Staten Island, it's because we are.

We make whatever we're in the mood for. And we're usually in the mood for *everything*. Despite the amount of food we make, there are hardly any leftovers. Last week, we went through seventy-five meatballs. Even by my family's standards, that's a lot of balls.

Meatballs by Ang

Simple, sinfully good meatballs:

1. Choose your ground meat. You can do beef, pork, or veal, or a combination of all. The fatter the meat, the better the taste.

2. Add a little chopped fresh basil, minced garlic, salt and pepper, bread crumbs or good Italian bread soaked in milk and then squeezed out. Sprinkle in some Romano cheese. Combine the ingredients (use your hands to mix really well).

3. Then roll into balls. I like a good size, somewhere between a golf and a squash ball. It fills the palm of my hand.

4. Heat olive oil in a pan. Cook balls, turning frequently, until done. *Mangia!*

Spanish Pork by Ang

This is a slow roast of the picnic cut—or the shoulder—of pork. Preheat oven to 200 degrees. Make a rub of adobo seasoning, saffron, garlic salt, salt, and pepper, then turn it into a paste with a little bit of water. Cover the pork with the paste. Put it in the oven. Roast it for twelve hours.

START EATING

If you come into my house, you must eat. Within five minutes of entering the front door, I will put a plate of food in front of you. When you leave my house, you'll be carrying a container with a stuffed artichoke or a wedge of Easter pie. If my guest says she's not hungry, or she just ate, this will not deter me. Even if you've just had a five-course dinner, there's always room for one more bite. "Just a little taste," I say, until my guest agrees. My version of "a little taste" is a full plate.

I feed people until their stomachs are on the verge of exploding. I've been accused of force-feeding them. Why? No matter how much people might protest, they lap it up (literally) and take obvious pleasure in it. When I see people eating and loving my food, it's total happiness. If you asked, "Would you rather cook for people or have sex?"—no hard and fast rule there, but I will say this: cooking is *always* satisfying.

Luger's Night

Every month or so, we have Peter Luger's Night at our house, an homage to the famous 125-year-old Brooklyn steak house. Their signature dish is a porterhouse steak— a thick T-bone cut with more tenderloin than loin. We broil it with butter, rare. Side dishes are creamed spinach, a wedge of iceberg with blue-cheese dressing, shrimp cocktail, and home-fried potatoes. For desert, ice cream sundaes with hot fudge.

DO A LOT WITH A LITTLE

I've always got a full fridge, freezer, and pantry. If there was a natural disaster, and we couldn't get to a supermarket, my family could survive for months on just what we've got at home. But if the cupboards were bare, I could still make an outstanding dish with just a few ingredients. All I need is garlic, olive oil, and a box of macaroni. No matter where I am, I keep these key three ingredients nearby. If I also have some bread crumbs and grated cheese, I can do wonders. If your car emergency kit doesn't include these three ingredients along with a tire iron and a spare, then you're not really prepared, are you? Better still, carry them in your purse!

Pasta e Olio by Ang

Boil water and cook the pasta.

While the pasta is cooking, sauté minced garlic in the oil until golden brown and soft. Toss the cooked pasta with the garlic and oil, and a little of the pasta water. Sprinkle with a grated-Parm-and-bread-crumb mixture. Salt and pepper to taste. *Buon appetito!*

NEVER SAY DIET

The day after a night of drinking martinis, I follow the Hangover Diet by going to Fortune Garden (salty, greasy, starchy Chinese food is an instant cure). If I go to a restaurant with a wiseguy, I stick to the Champagne and Lobster Diet and order the most expensive items on the menu. If I'm having an early meal before a party night, I follow the No Greens Diet. (Do *not* mix anything green—Caesar salad, sautéed broccoli rabe, spinach—with a lot of alcohol. You will throw up.) Otherwise, I do not diet.

If I haven't made this point already, food is a source of joy, not something to feel guilty about. Eating is pleasure, not punishment. Refusing a beautiful plate of food made by a family member or just nibbling at steak prepared by my favorite chef would be an insult and a waste. Avoiding margaritas or swearing off lasagna to lose weight? Never. So what if you can fit into smaller jeans? You'll be the same person— except hungrier and bitchier.

TAKE IT SLOW

Fast food? Forget it! Even if I'm in a rush and want something quick, I go to a real sandwich shop, like Dom's, for good, quality ingredients. Think quality, not speed. I'll go to a place that looks shady on the outside—and the inside—but if the food is delicious, just *try* to keep me out.

THE FASTEST WAY TO A
MAN'S WALLET . . .

. . . is through his stomach, of course.

Now that Neil and I are making a go of it, my dating

days are behind me. But when I was single, I never had a problem getting dates, and I never will. In part, it's because of my skills in the kitchen. I don't care who the man is, how old, of whatever ethnicity or background. If a woman can prepare a juicy steak, he'll fall for her. Wiseguys in particular are seduced by a pretty pasta puttanesca. They have a soft spot in their hearts for any woman who can make Italian dishes like their mama used to. If you can, you might as well start shopping for a new fur coat.

When I used to invite a wiseguy over for dinner, the food was the star. Well, no, actually, I was the star. I wore a hot outfit and looked amazing, but the food definitely ran a close second. I set the table by loading it down with heaping platters of hot dishes. If the meal was for two, I cooked for six. Ambience? Meh. All that stuff that people do, dimming the lights, playing soft music, putting out flowers? Whatever. That's not me. I'm not a romantic person in a cliché, predictable way. Anyone can light a freakin' candle and scatter rose petals. But not a lot of women can do what I do to a pork cutlet.

A sample date-night menu:

APPETIZER. I'd start with a fish dish, something light but spicy. I've made a seafood salad of octopus, shrimp, crab, lobster, calamari, and scungilli tossed with lemon juice, garlic, olive oil, parsley, and red pepper. I love red pepper. It goes on everything. Bring the heat!

MAIN COURSE. Wiseguys want red meat. If I served a vegetarian dish as the main course, they'd probably get up and drive straight to the nearest steak house. I couldn't do without meat, either. I'd give up beef, pork, and chicken exactly one day before I'd keel over and die. One of my absolute favorite flavors is the marrow from a veal shank. You dig it out with a tiny spoon, add a little salt, and spread it on toast. Yummy. So, yeah, men like something to tear apart with their teeth. A porterhouse or New York strip, grilled. A fried pork cutlet, or chicken cutlet. A grilled lobster. My steak pizzaiola has brought grown men—big, tough guys—to tears. I serve either bread or pasta (linguine and clams, or macaroni and gravy), and a vegetable or salad with it. If I can't decide what to do, I make it all.

WINE. Always *vino* with dinner. With red meat, I'd pour a Jordan cabernet from the Sonoma Valley in California. It's like drinking velvet. With fish, I like La Scolca Gavi di Gavi Black Label, an Italian white that pops on the tongue. I pour my wine into a crystal carafe to breathe twenty minutes or so before we eat.

DESSERT. I do not bake. I've never cared to learn how to do it. Why bother when I can rely on to-die-for pastries from my baker friends, like my old pal Baby John DeLutro, the undisputed Cannoli King of New York. At Caffe Palermo on Mulberry Street in Little Italy, he makes them fresh, with ricotta cream, and each bite is freakin' heaven.

DO *NOT* GO GARDEN FRESH

Every cook knows the benefit of fresh ingredients. Pastene canned tomatoes make a nice gravy, but fresh tomatoes are even better. So I decided last year that I was going to grow my own. I dug up a square of lawn and turned it into a vegetable patch. Along with eleven plum cherry tomato plants, I put in mint, basil, and parsley.

I was a model gardener. Like a good mama, I spoiled the little plants. They wanted water? Fertilizer? I couldn't say no to my babies. I made sure they were comfortable and tilled the soil. I kept them well groomed by pulling out weeds and trimming the dry leaves.

And the babies flourished. They grew and grew. I was so proud of them, and myself. When the plants put out their first tomatoes, I jumped up and down and clapped my hands for joy. And then, they put up more tomatoes. And more. And more. I started to have tomatoes up the freakin' ass. Every time I turned around, another fifty of them appeared. They started falling off the vine. And that attracted squirrels and rodents.

It was an unholy *nightmare*. I was making fresh gravy

three times a week for six months. I was giving it away to my family, my friends. If you walked by my house, I'd chase you down on the street with a huge Tupperware container of gravy.

By the fall, I was tomatoed out. When the plants finally died, I didn't have a funeral. I threw a party. Never again. That's why, in my new house, there will not be one foot of grass and not a single bit of dirt. I'm paving over the lawn and putting out a pot with a big plastic tree.

10
Big Family Rules

ithout a doubt, the biggest—and most important—thing in my large life is my tremendous family. My relatives by blood or marriage number in the hundreds. I could do a family tree, but it'd take a forest's worth of paper to print it. My mom had six siblings and I have six siblings, and they all have families, including my sister Janine, who has seven kids. I have twenty-five first cousins, and they have kids, and so on. You'd think it would be a lot to keep track of. But we don't fall out of touch. We're always in each other's houses and business (personal and professional). We don't go a day (or, in some cases, an hour) without checking in, on the phone or in person.

In a few weeks, after we move into the mansion, I'll be under one roof again with my immediate family: my daughter,

Raquel; her son/my grandson, Sal; my son, A.J.; and Neil, my husband of three years. Nearly all my siblings, nieces, and nephews are only a fifteen-minute drive away. The constant stream of family members through our house has been a huge adjustment for Neil. But he just had to get used to it. This is how I like it, and the only way of life I've known.

66 The first time I met Ang's mother, Jean, it was Christmas Eve. She was cooking a seven-course Italian seafood dinner, in her bra, with a cigarette in her mouth. People were coming in and out, and Jean talked to them all, but kept right on cooking. Everyone in neighborhood ate at that table. I just fell in love with Jean on sight. She was a real Italian mama."

—Little Jenn, friend

REMEMBER WHERE YOU COME FROM

My parents, Jean and Sonny, met through Mom's friend Frankie. Mom was nineteen at the time, and Dad was thirty-nine. The twenty-year age difference couldn't have been easy.

Their marriage was rough from the start. They fought each other tooth and nail. I remember that they argued constantly, but I've blocked out the specific fights. I hated listening to that. My "no fighting" philosophy probably dates back to watching their marriage. When they'd start arguing, I'd go into my room, crank the radio to drown them out, or jump out the window to meet up with friends.

I wouldn't say my childhood was deprived. We had food on the table and a house to live in. But there was not a lot of money—or attention—to spread around. (We certainly didn't have millions of dollars in a safe under the floorboards, or businesses to hand out like meatball heroes to all the kids.) If I wanted any of the extras—clothes, makeup, cash for going out—I'd have to work for it. I got my first job as a bartender at the Nineteenth Hole, a mob hangout, when I was fifteen. I walked in there and told the manager I'd been helping out my parents, who were both bartenders, for years. "I know what I'm doing," I said.

The guy who hired me looked me over. "How old are you?" he asked, cigar in the corner of his mouth.

"Eighteen." That was the legal drinking age in New York back then.

I have no idea if he believed me. But he seemed satisfied with my lie. I looked older than I was and carried myself with enough attitude to fool him. And I looked pretty damn good behind that bar. Business picked up as soon as I started working there.

      I'm two years older than Ang. I remember her as a cute little kid. She was good, until she was a teenager. That's when she got wild. When she was twelve or thirteen, she came home with a Big Ang tattoo on her leg. Our father went wacko. Can't tell you how many times Dad left the house and came back, yelling, 'Where's my fucking car? My car was stolen.' It was gone, though, because Ang went out the window at night, took his car, and drove all over Brooklyn with her friends."

—*Ronald, brother*

MOM RULES THE ROOST

My mom was tough. She was always keeping the kids in line, doing whatever she had to do for her family. Seven nights a week, she worked as a bartender, like my dad. When my parents weren't working at the bar, they were busy at the house, taking care of the business of life. With seven kids, there was a lot to do. Mom was constantly cooking and cleaning. The amount of laundry that woman did—unbelievable. I definitely got my work ethic from her. Mom never stopped. As far as she was concerned, sleep was for babies.

Her nickname was Machine Gun Jean because she was so protective of her family and anyone she cared about. She was tough, and not very affectionate. But she'd do anything for her kids—and our friends.

66 I remember one night, Ang and I slept at her mom's after a long night of partying. At dawn, my boyfriend woke up the whole house by screaming and banging on the door, acting crazy, demanding to see me (he was pissed that we left him behind at the club).

"Jean answered the door in her robe and, calm as day, said, 'What can I do for you?'

"My boyfriend made a commotion, ranting about see-ing me *right now*. Jean said calmly, 'I'll let you into my house. But if you do one thing to that girl, I'll kill you.'

"This big tough guy knew she meant it. He instantly quieted down, lowered his eyes, and said, 'Yes, ma'am.' "

—Celia, friend

KNOW WHEN TO CALL
IT QUITS

After twenty-five years of rocky marriage, my parents divorced when I was sixteen. I was glad. Yes, divorce isn't something to aspire to. But they'd put each other through enough hell. It was a good call to end the marriage.

Mom took up with John, the man who became my stepfather. I'm taking an omertà on talking about him. Suffice it to say, I thought he was a jerk-off, so I stayed at my dad's house. Janine and one of our brothers lived with Mom and John. He owned a liquor store and did well, so Mom didn't have to work again. My sister Janine was the baby of the family and was around nine when Mom stopped working. We older siblings always said Janine got a different mother from the rest of us. Mom was a lot more relaxed when she didn't have to work nights. She stopped yelling, for one thing.

DON'T TAKE YOUR PARENTS
FOR GRANTED

My Mom and John moved to a condo in Florida when I was in my mid-twenties. She came to visit her kids in Brooklyn, and she wanted all of us to return to Florida with her for an extended visit. Janine's baby was six months old, so she couldn't go. My other siblings had one excuse or another. But I was up for it. Raquel was a baby at the time. I took her down South with me. I remember we arrived on a Wednesday.

That Friday, two days later, Mom took some laundry to the machines down the hall from her condo. I heard a loud thump and thought, "What was that?" My stepfather and I ran out and found my mom on the floor in the hallway. My stepfather got down there and cradled her head, calling her name and asking what was wrong. Mom said, "I can't see you."

The ambulance came and she was taken to the hospital. She fell into a coma and stayed on a respirator for two days. The doctors told us she'd had an aneurysm, and that the damage was severe. She'd never recover or wake up. Her brain was gone. By now, most of my siblings and some uncles had come. We had to decide whether to take her off the machines. Mom was fifty-six when she died.

> 66 Ang was devastated. For the first couple of days, she was the only one of the siblings there, and it was all on her to deal with the situation. My husband, Sally, flew down and saw that all of Jean's kids were out of it, just so upset. The decision to take her off life support was incredibly hard to make. That event changed Ang's whole life and her way of thinking. She lost her mother at an early age. As close as our family is—the closest—she learned she had to depend on herself. One way or another, she had to support herself and her children. You do what you gotta do."
>
> —Rita, aunt

EVEN IF YOU THINK YOU CAN'T HANDLE SOMETHING, YOU CAN

One day, Mom was doing laundry, the next, gone. The sight of her in the hallway is etched in my memory, and it devastates me whenever I think of it. I try not to, but the image comes up when I least expect it, and I relive the moment like it just happened. She'd never been sick, and she was so young when she passed. No one could have ever predicted that my mom, who was so full of life, would die so suddenly. The light just went out. It was a shock. I'm still shocked, twenty-five years later.

After Mom died, I just couldn't handle the idea that I was living in a world that didn't include her. I started to get panic attacks. They'd come on fast. Out of nowhere, my vision would blur. I couldn't breathe. I thought I was having a heart attack. If you've never had one, I can tell you that panic attacks are terrifying. I genuinely believed I was dying every time it happened. My sister helped me deal with them by slipping me half a Xanax. I'm not a pill person, but I have to admit, that shit worked.

The panic attacks subsided. I still get flare-ups, though. My sadness about not having a mom does not go away. I still cry from missing her all the time, but never more so than when I was a young, single mom, and her guidance and advice would have helped me tremendously. Raquel would get sick, and I'd reach for the phone to call my Mom and remember she was gone. When A.J. got into trouble as a teenager, I wished I could have called my Mom to ask her how she put up with me. More than anything, I wish she'd been there when Sal was born. He's so precious and sweet. I kept imagining her among the family at the hospital that night, taking turns holding the baby, her great-grandson. It breaks my heart that Mom never got to know my kids or Sal.

WHEN YOUR PARENTS ARE BOTH DEAD, YOU'RE ON YOUR OWN

Dad followed Mom a few years later, at age seventy-nine. He had a long history of heart disease. In his last year, he also suffered with Alzheimer's. Because of his health history, his death wasn't as much of a shock as Mom's. But it was, of course, awful.

Even though I was in my mid-twenties by then, had been living on my own, and was already a mother myself, I mark the death of my parents as the beginning of my life as an independent woman—and I was not happy about it. I was miserable about losing them. Mom was the glue that held the family together. We all went wacko for a while after she passed. And then Dad was gone, too. I wasn't ready to support myself without their guidance and help. The unglued feeling was compounded because none of my brothers were available to me (for various reasons, including being behind bars), either.

My brother-in-law, Janine's husband, Dominick, stepped up as the man of the family. Janine and I were both wrecked about the deaths, and Dom was tremendous for both of us. He is more like a brother to me than a brother-in-law. And Janine is far more than a sister. She's my best friend and my personal adviser. I don't make a move without talking to her first. We're on the phone constantly. If she's in trouble, I run over there. Or, more likely, if I'm in some kind of trouble, she comes right to me. No matter how much they help me, though, at the end of the day, I knew I was responsible for my kids and myself, and that I'd do what I had to do to support us. I found a lot of strength moving forward on my own, knowing Janine and Dom had my back.

❝ The siblings are all very close, especially Ang and Janine. They always were. It's odd to say, but losing their mother young tightened the bond between them. When Janine and I first got together, Ang would take all the kids—Janine had kids from before we met—and make it possible for us to get time alone. She's helped us move, pack and unpack. Whenever she can pitch in, she does.

"When their parents died within a few years of each other, all of the brothers were incarcerated. I was the only man in the family who wasn't. Ang was a single mom, and I'm glad I was in the position to help out. Sometimes, it was giving her money, or moving her in with us, dealing with car trouble, personal-life trouble. We sold houses and went on vacations together. Ang always returned the favor. The family attitude is that you do whatever you can for each other, according to your ability and talents."

—*Dominick, brother-in-law*

FAMILY STAYS TOGETHER BEYOND THE GRAVE

My mom was dead for seventeen years when my brother Louis and I decided to disinter her and have her buried with our father. We had a vote. Some of the siblings didn't agree with the decision, but we all chipped in to do it anyway. It cost $5,000. Why do it? It was more convenient for the living to visit them right next to each other. And, whatever their problems, they *were* married for twenty-five years and had seven kids and over a dozen grandkids. I liked the idea of them being together, finally at peace, at rest, beyond the grave. And now they are.

SHOW, DON'T TELL

My parents weren't affectionate or expressive about their feelings for us. I admit, I have a hard time saying how I feel. But my family understands how much they mean to me. I try to show it every day through my cooking, how hard I work to support them. I take them everywhere and keep them close. That Raquel and A.J. want to stay close to me says it all. The message is getting through.

11
Big Motherhood Rules

I'm every kind of mother there is: a mother, grandmother, stepmother, godmother, and "den mother" to my *Mob Wives* castmates. My mom was the glue that held our family together, the one who stuck to our traditions. And now it's my turn to take over. Keeping family connected and caring for the kids with as much determination as my mom had is the highest aspiration I could have as a parent.

> ❝ I never got to meet my grandmother. I hear that she was a great person who'd help anyone and loved to cook and throw parties. Ang figured, after her mom died, that she'd pick up where Grandma left off."
>
> —A.J., son

THERE WILL BE PAIN

Although I'd spent plenty of time with kids, I didn't know what I was getting myself into when I got pregnant. But labor and delivery? Freakin' *nightmare*.

When I was pregnant with Raquel in 1985, I acted like my life wasn't going to change because of a baby. I put in my regular hours at the bar until I was nine months pregnant. I was working when I went into labor with her. It was in the middle of winter during a raging storm with snow up to your ass. I had no idea how much contractions were going to hurt. My boyfriend drove me to the hospital. Between my screams and the snow, he almost crashed three times. I went through twelve hours of grueling, agonizing labor. I screamed nonstop. I think other patients might've run for their lives, hearing me shrieking my head off like in *The Exorcist*.

My voice is still recovering from that night.

Raquel was a beautiful baby, though. She's named after Raquel Welch, my favorite movie star. I brought my baby home and felt pretty relaxed—for about five minutes. Then the crying started. She had colic. For four months, she was like a little terrorist, wailing hysterically for hours and hours every day and night. It was torture. But when she finally shut up already, she was adorable—and so serious, even as an infant.

I loved her so much that four years later, I gave her a brother.

One night, the kids' father and I went out to dinner with another couple. The girlfriend said, "Let's go dancing!" I was always up for that, even seven months pregnant, but my boyfriend wasn't. He went home and I went to Pastels, the disco in Bay Ridge. I was partying with my friends when suddenly my water broke. Right there on the dance floor, with the music blaring and the lights flashing. The other dancers probably thought someone spilled a drink. A really big drink. I was shocked. I was wearing a Michael Jackson–style white jacket with studs and rhinestones, and a pair of white leggings. I looked down and saw that the leggings were stained and soaking. This wasn't supposed to happen. I still had seven weeks to go. I had to scream over the music to tell my friends what had happened, pointing at my dripping legs and feet. "My! Water! Just! Broke!"

"What?" one asked. "You want a Coke?"

"MY WATER JUST BROKE!!!"

My voice is still recovering from that night, too.

Eventually, my friends got me to the hospital. Two hours later, Anthony Jean, named after my paternal grandfather and my mom, was born. There wasn't nearly as much agony the second time around. A.J. was a sweet baby from day one. Not colicky at all. He loved to laugh and snuggle. He was so good, a mama's boy until thirteen. And then he became a man and stopped being such an angel.

     When I had Sonnie, now twelve, Ang was in the delivery room. She'd had two kids by then, but hadn't seen a baby being born before. The whole time, she was asking me, 'Why aren't you screaming?' When Ang was in labor, she screamed loud enough to raise the dead bodies in the hospital morgue. I just lie there and don't say a word. I have high tolerance for pain. Ang? The opposite! But she puts up with it if she knows the potential outcome is worth any pain she might experience in the meantime. That holds up for her about everything, from labor to plastic surgery to relationships to businesses."

—Janine, sister

SPOIL THE KIDS

My *Mob Wives* costars Karen, Renee, and Ramona have talked about being Mafia princesses when they were young. As kids, they were given extravagant gifts and parties. Wherever they went in the five boroughs, they could say their father's name to get drinks and access. Karen was given her own flower shop when she graduated high school.

I didn't have any of that. (For that matter, I didn't graduate high school.) My parents weren't in a position to dole out a lot of money or time to their kids. Even if my parents made big bucks, with seven kids there were just too many of us to spoil.

As soon as I became a mother, though, I felt the urge to shower my kids with gifts and clothes. I set out to spoil them, big-time. I have to work my ass off to do it, and I haven't always managed to give Raquel and A.J. the life I'd like them to have. But I've come pretty close. Spoiling them is my prime directive. It gets me up each day and fills my dreams at night. I drove them to school every morning. I bought them trendy clothes, took them on vacations, paid for cars. Whatever they want, I give. If A.J. wants a loan to open a pizzeria in Florida—he's been talking about that—I'll write the check. I might roll my eyes at him a few times to test his commitment. But he knows I'm a soft touch.

I'm sure parenting experts out there would say that

giving your kid whatever he wants would wreck his character, make him feel entitled, and destroy his work ethic. I don't care what people think. I've been doing it this way for twenty-seven years, and my kids turned out pretty great. Raquel is a knockout. The best-looking seventh-grade special-ed teacher in the world, probably. And she gave me Sal, my gorgeous grandson, the love of my life.

Raquel has always been a serious person, and she probably thinks I should have been more like she is now when I was a young mother. It's true that, for a lot of her childhood, she had to take care of A.J. when I worked at night. I did put the responsibility on her. That forced her to be a kind of mom when she was still a kid herself. At the time, she might've resented it. But it's also one of the reasons she's so great with kids, and such an excellent teacher and mother now.

I'm deeply proud of her. Our relationship is one of equals. We argue and bicker a lot. My friends tell me it's hilarious to listen to. I can hear our conversations outside my head sometimes and just laugh at how much we sound like an old married couple. Running underneath the back-and-forth, though, is mutual respect. Since she's a single working mom herself, Raquel and I understand each other perfectly, even when we argue.

As for A.J., well, he's my baby. Sons in the Italian culture are put on a pedestal. They're the princes. I definitely treated A.J. that way. We're close. I'm overprotective of him in a way

I never was with Raquel. Thank God he's not interested in the mob lifestyle, much to my relief. He pays his bills, works hard at his job. He's not serious with any girls, but a lot of girls are crazy for him. They should be. He's gorgeous!

B.J.

" Anything that goes wrong, Mom is right there to help. I had a couple of health issues as a kid and once needed surgery. Mom did not leave my side for a second. When I first got a two-wheeler, I didn't know how to ride it, but I jumped on and flew straight down a steep hill. I crashed and got deep cuts on my whole side. It looked like I fell off a motorcycle. Mom ran down the hill and patched me up. She's been running down the hill to take care of me for my whole life, and I don't see that stopping."

—A.J., son

Raquel and A.J. are hard workers, like me. Responsible. They're living proof that kids turn out okay, grow up to have good ethics, even if you buy them things and take them on lavish trips. If I didn't spoil my family, what else am I going to do with my time and money?

66 She calls me a mama's boy. I definitely am. It's all about
Mama. I have her name tattooed over my heart for that
reason. Mom always made sure we had the best of everything. She took care of us and never wanted to see us sad.
If I was sad, she'd do something to change my mind-set,
like make me something to eat, or just sit and talk, and
tell me it wasn't that bad. A lot of mothers and sons don't
talk that much. But Mom always talked out my problems
with me, without judgment. She always tried to get to the
bottom of it. Of course, we have had a few fights. But it
was minimal. Her philosophy is that there's always a better solution than arguing."

—A.J., son

SPOIL THE GODKIDS

In the Catholic faith, the godmother stands up at the baby's
christening, the baptism ceremony in church. The rule is, if
the parents were to pass, the godmother is responsible for the
child's religious education. I'm a godmother of six kids. It's
kind of ridiculous that I'd be anyone's spiritual leader. When
I go to church, my brain goes numb. I sit there for hours, and
when I walk out, I can't even remember being there. It's like

God gave me a noogie. So instead of concerning myself with my godchildren's faith, I work on their fashion.

> " Ang as a spiritual leader? I'm scared."
>
> —*Janine, sister*

> " I love having Ang as my aunt! She's always trendy, and she stays up on what's happening with clothes or music. It's not that she's trying to stay young or is like one of those women who dresses like a kid. She just loves new things and wants to be current. And we go on epic shopping trips together to the Short Hills Mall."
>
> —*Jeannie, niece*

ALL THE KIDS ARE MY KIDS

My five-year-old nephew, Ronnie, calls me Grandma. My thirty-year-old nephew, Ronnie, calls me Aunt Ang, but he might as well call me Mom. All of my siblings' children might as well be my own kids. Janine feels the same way about

Raquel and A.J. We've raised our children together, have been at their side every step of the way. Not just the major days, like birthdays and graduations. We're there *every* day.

> " Ang is more than just an aunt. She's also done a lot for me and my sister and brother. When we were kids, we'd walk to her place—she lived only a couple of blocks away—to eat and hang out. I used to babysit my cousins when Ang had to go to work. She took care of us, and I took care of A.J. and Raquel. That's what it's like to be part of this family. We're always having fun together, and taking care of each other. Now that we're older, we go to the Beach Club and drink all day, or go to Fortune Garden and drink all night."
>
> —*Ronnie, nephew*

KIDS SHOULD HAVE A LONG LEASH

I've never punished my kids. No time-outs. I didn't ground them or yell at them. My parents tried it with me. I was a trouble magnet as a teenager, and my parents busted me constantly. Punishment doesn't work, though. Dad tried to lock me in, but I'd just go out the window anyway. I was compelled to break out. I hated sitting still or being stuck in the house. I wanted to get out there, dance, go to bars, and meet people. I loved action and adventure. If something was going on, I wanted to be there.

All moms make adjustments to how their parents did things. I didn't want my kids to jump out the window, so I didn't lock them in. They have gotten into trouble over the years, absolutely. But they also faced up to it and got out of it on their own, without me coming down on them. I'm here to help them when they get in trouble, not to make it worse.

We have argued, though. I remember having a fight with Raquel about cigarettes. She said to me, "I don't smoke!" while smoke was coming out of her mouth!

You put too many rules on kids, they'll want to break them. It's human nature, especially in my family. Resisting authority runs deep. So my parenting theory was that if you're not strict and demanding, kids rebel by putting the restrictions and demands on themselves. Raquel and A.J. were amazing students and didn't get in with a bad crowd in high school, either. So my theory held up.

> " Ang was the coolest mom in the neighborhood. We hung out at her house. We could do what we wanted there, smoke or whatever. She didn't mind. It wasn't like she was trying to be our friend, or a 'cool mom.' She just *is* cool, and she *is* like a mother to me. I felt like part of the family. I basically grew up there, had countless dinners, confided my problems to her more than I did to my own mother. It says a lot that we're all extremely close still. Once you're part of the family, you're in it for life."
>
> —Ryan, Raquel's best friend

I've always given my kids a long leash. A lot longer than my dogs! A.J. especially loves his freedom, with his twenty-three girlfriends—as he joked on the show, "One for each year of my life." Sooner or later he'll meet a nice girl to take care of him. He can't expect me to do it forever—although, if push came to shove, he knows I would. Whoever A.J. settles down with, I'm sure she'll put him on a much shorter leash than I ever did. Meanwhile, I can't wait for him to move back home to the new house with his mother, where he belongs.

> ❝ I'm looking forward to moving back in with Mom. I really haven't been around a lot the last couple of years. We'd talk on the phone constantly, and I'd see Mom and Raquel whenever I could. But being together again is what I want now. I'd like to be there when my nephew's growing up. When I was young, I was really close with my older guy cousins. They'd come over to babysit when Mom was working at night, and I looked up to them as my brothers. It never bothered me that Mom worked so much at night. She always made sure someone we liked was there. I want to be like that for Sal."
>
> —A.J., son

SPOIL THE STEPKIDS

When I married Neil, I became a stepmother, too. It must have been awkward for Brianna to be introduced to a stranger and to be expected to think of her as a kind of mother. I thought Brianna was lovely and sweet from the start and gave her my usual treatment of indulgence and attention. I bought her gifts, took her shopping, got her to help in the kitchen. I wore down her shyness bit by bit, and now she's like one of my own, too.

66 At first, Ang was intimidating. My father had started seeing her more and more, and I didn't think anything serious
was going on. I started going to the bar and family parties. The family is so big, and there are so many of them
to remember. I'm not as loud and out there as the rest
of them. I'd sit in the corner and not talk too much. But
if you're shy, Ang will put a stop to that. If I was over for
dinner and sitting by myself texting, Ang would say, 'Go
upstairs and hang out with the girls.' She forces you to
open up and have fun.

"Ang made me feel comfortable. And now that I've
gotten used it, it's incredible to be a part of her family.
She's awesome. Whatever my dad says no to, Ang says
yes. All my friends love her because she's fun, never in a
bad mood. And if she is, it doesn't affect anyone else. She
vents and it's over."

—*Brianna, stepdaughter*

DOUBLE-SPOIL THE GRANDKIDS

No one is more important than my grandson. Just one look at
Sal's beautiful face, and my heart gets tight. He is my top pri-
ority from the minute I wake up—literally. Every morning, he

climbs into my bed and gets between Neil and me. (My husband doesn't love it, but too bad.) I get out of bed, make Sal pastini with butter and salt, give him a bath, get him dressed, and take him to school. Our mornings are the best part of my day.

I buy Sal whatever he wants—toys, clothes. If he asks for it, he gets it, period. I'll cook for him any time of the day or night. Candy? Snacks? Anything his heart desires.

Raquel gets angry with me for spoiling him. Sal knows that if he comes to me, I'm going to say yes, and if he goes to Raquel, she has to say no. So she winds up being the bad guy, the disciplinarian. But, I figure, since she's a teacher, she knows how to do it the right way. And since I'm the grandmother, it's my prerogative to spoil him. Raquel can't complain too much about my lax rules. I'm a permanent babysitter for her—and she'd never find a better one.

““ When I was giving birth to Sal, there were thirty people in the delivery room. Fifteen people by the door. Fifteen in the room. When you're in labor, the last thing you want is dozens of people staring at you. I just wanted my mom! My boyfriend said, 'And I just want my mom.' And if two or three people are in the room, then everyone else wants to get in there, too.

"Mom coached me through it, stayed positive even when I was freaking out. I had trouble breathing at one point and was put in an oxygen tent. Everyone was getting nervous because the baby wasn't coming out. But eventually he did. And then there was a huge celebration in the delivery room and the waiting room. The hospital staff had never seen anything like it before. The newborn was passed between thirty people. Someone was videotaping it. It was the middle of winter, and Uncle Dom showed up in shorts and flip-flops, totally ossified. And then, just to add to the excitement, an elevator shaft in the hospital caught on fire, and everyone had to evacuate and run for the exits. Having a baby is a pretty big deal, always a drama, for anyone. But in my family? Quadruple it."

—Raquel, daughter

When Sal was eight or nine months old, not yet walking, I took him to Mommy and Me classes on Forest Avenue in Staten Island with Janine and her son Ronnie and my friend Denise and her granddaughter, who was the same age. It was a crazy scene, all the mothers and grandmothers sitting in a circle, singing kid songs and clapping along while the babies in our laps were asleep or crying or clueless about what was going on. Honestly, I don't know how much Sal got out of it. But I loved it. It was fun to do it with friends. Also, just being able to spend time with Sal like this, as the mommy, felt like a privilege, or even a second chance. When my kids were babies, I was a single working mother, tending bar until four in the morning, supporting us on my own, always stressed out. Now, with Sal, I get to do those mommy things.

A month ago, I took him to Disney World in Orlando for a week. We went with a group of eighteen people—friends, family, and their kids (you might've figured out by now, we tend to travel in a pack). The whole group had dinner together every night, but in the morning, we all went our separate ways with our own kids. Sal and I strolled around the park together. Everything that a three-year-old needs done, I did for him. This was right around the time I was starting to get noticed for being on television, and people would stop me to take my picture. I'd keep one hand on the stroller and smile for the camera. Sal didn't understand why complete strangers wanted to take my picture. He probably thinks it's because I'm the World's Greatest Grandma.

KNOW WHEN TO BE A PUSHOVER, AND WHEN TO PUSH BACK

If you figure this one out, fill me in. I don't have a clue.

12

Big Friendship Rules

Second only to my family are my friends. I've known most of them since before I had a family of my own. These people have been in my life for so long, I can't imagine a world without them. They're more than friends. They're lifers. For us, friendship is a life sentence, in the best way. My friends halve my pain and double my joy. And I hope that I do the same for them.

> 66 We grew up together and ran with the same group of friends for thirty-plus years. It's our own crew. My father, Sally Dogs, used to say he'd rather have our crew backing him. We were the sharp ones, us girls."
>
> —*Sallyann, cousin*

FRIENDSHIP IS FOREVER

On *Mob Wives*, there was so much drama between Karen and Drita over the definition of friendship. In a nutshell, Karen believes that once you form a friendship, you're solid for life. Drita believes in a more active relationship, that a friendship has to be maintained. You can't drop out of someone's life for months and expect to classify as "close."

My definition is a combination of both. Once you're my friend, you are "in" for life *and* the relationship should be active and involved. It's not so hard to maintain friendships. Just pick up the phone. Send a text. Stop by the bar. Bring a six-pack to a friend's house. Throw a party and make sure they're invited.

My ability to stay in touch might be because I don't like to be alone. When I do find myself in an empty house—which is not often—I call someone. I like action, conversation, and connecting with people. I'm always wondering what's going on in the world without me—so I make the call to find out. And when I make plans, I keep them. My crew and I do everything together—shopping, prison visits, cooking, beauty treatments, travel. I'd be lost at sea without them. Friendships aren't obligations. They're touchstones, and that's more valuable than gemstones.

DON'T DO DRAMA

I lost any tolerance for loud fights listening to my parents when I was a kid. So now, when I hear women in screaming matches with their so-called friends, I pivot on my stiletto and leave. If you love and care for someone, why the hell would you want to shriek at each other like caged gorillas? A close pal hurts your feelings? Then explain yourself quietly and rationally. Don't go ballistic!

I have to shake my head in disbelief at the verbal attacks and tension between the women on *Mob Wives*. It's out of control. These are grown women with kids who act like kids themselves, throwing tantrums, threatening, and yelling at each other over bullshit. I can't stand it. Most of the fights are about a dig one of the others allegedly said, or something she might or might not have done in the past. If the conflict happened years ago, forget it. What's done is done. You can't change the past, so let the problem roll off your back. And then move the fuck *on*.

All the screaming is a waste of time, energy, and breath. Instead of screaming, they could be laughing. As Drita said on the show, she'd rather laugh all day than get in a stupid fight. *Me, too.*

GET OVER IT!

I try to be a peacemaker. If two of my friends are having a disagreement, I stay neutral, urge them to sit down, talk it out, come to terms, or agree to disagree. And then, repeat after me: *GET OVER IT!* Calm the fuck down. Relax. Let bygones be bygones. Otherwise, you're living in an unhealthy state of anxiety and tension. How happy can you be if you want to rip someone's throat open?

To iron out grievances, I recommend a Happy Hour Consult with a couple of impartial players in the mix to keep things on the right track and under control. This usually works. If the warring parties can't come to terms, the next best thing is to dig a hole and bury the conflict. Call a truce, and try to pick up the friendship from there. If that's not possible, then just stay out of each other's way. You don't bother me, and I don't bother you.

I admit, at times my peacemaking efforts have backfired. The most public example was when I tried to broker a peace between Karen and Drita at Renee's Celebration of Life party at the beginning of *Mob Wives* season two. I encouraged them to have a talk, and it felt like an ambush to one woman and an attack to another. In hindsight, I guess it wasn't the right setting or time to smooth things over. I could be depressed about that. Or, I could shrug it off, know my intention was honorable, and *get over it*. And, if you can't get over it, then you should probably ask yourself if your intentions really were honorable. The real issue might be guilt.

> 66 If I complain to Ang that I regret something I did, she says, 'Did you have fun? Yeah? Then get over it.' It's not only that she's forgiving and doesn't judge other people harshly. She doesn't want you to be a harsh judge of yourself."
>
> —Ryan, Raquel's best friend

DON'T GOSSIP

I wouldn't have to put out fires if my friends didn't spark them off in the first place. The easiest, best way to avoid She Said, She Said violent battles? Keep your mouth shut. Don't dump on someone who's not there to set the record straight. If you have nothing better to do than trash someone behind her back, she's not the bitch. You are.

PRIDE IS FOR LOSAHS

My best friends have been in my life forever. We have history. They're not people I just met last year who I don't trust. I do think you gotta keep your guard up with new people. You never know if they're going to stab you in the back. I've been there before.

But with old friendships that have been tested by the trials of life—after decades together, you know all too well who's really got your back—there is simply no point in arguing. You love this person; she loves you. If there's a misunderstanding, then get to the bottom of it. Sit down with a bottle of wine and talk through it. Keep the wild emotions in check. I try to deflate the tension by making people laugh. And I always apologize to smooth things over. Being too proud to say "I'm sorry" can destroy friendships. My friendships are more precious than my pride.

SPOIL THE FRIENDS

I love buying gifts for my friends. As soon as I get a dollar in my pocket, I'm out the door to find a cute present for my crew. My ratio for purchases is about two to one. For every two items I buy for myself, I get one for someone else—my kids, or my crew. This is why I wind up spending $10,000 a

year at Christmas. Recently, while I was in Florida, I went on a mini–spending spree and found the cutest silver flasks with a pink leather cover that read GIRL'S NIGHT OUT. I bought a dozen of them and doled them out to my girls when I got home.

> " I remember going to Ang's house, and there was this homeless man having dinner at her table. Leroy had no teeth, lived in a Dumpster. He was hungry, so Ang brought him home for a meal. Ang doesn't see color or class. She lets anyone into her home, sees the good in everyone, and thinks everyone is her friend. I worry about that sometimes. Her generosity and being the least judgmental person on the planet makes her naive, in a way. People can take advantage. I want to smack her sometimes for trusting everyone. It's gotten her into trouble in the past."
>
> —Donna, sister

“ Ang is the most generous friend. She loves to buy presents, and then she gets really excited about giving them to people and can't wait to see how they react when they open them. It's Christmas all year with Ang. Lately, it's gotten to the point where she doesn't even bother shopping by herself and wrapping gifts. She just takes her friends, or A.J. and Raquel, right to the store and buys them whatever they want. And maybe she'll pick up something for herself, too.

"And Ang cannot keep a gift a secret. It bursts out of her. Can't tell you how many times she's said to me, 'I just bought you a present for your birthday next month. But you're not getting it until then, and I'm not telling you what it is.'

"Then I say, 'What is it?'

"And she goes, 'Oh, fuck it. Here it is! Open it up *right now*.' "

—Celia, friend

THROW PARTIES, NOT PUNCHES

Even if you *know* you're being crossed, that doesn't mean you should start a brawl like a testosterone-pumped jerk-off. I just don't get why women want to fight like tough guys. They

might as well *be* men. That is just not my style. I've never thrown a punch in my life. For one thing, I might break a nail. For another, it's unladylike. I cross my legs. I don't kick with them. Guys don't like it when women fight. I also think it's bad for kids to see their parents fight—with each other, or anyone else. It leaves a bad impression on them. If they see Mommy throw a punch, then they think it's okay for them to do it.

❝ Mom and I always had different ways of seeing things. I'm like the mother, and she's the daughter. I think she's way too carefree. She doesn't take things seriously enough. She's forgiving to her friends—to a fault. She'd let too many people into our house. They were always coming around to hang out or for parties. Then, we'd go on vacation, come home, and the place would be cleaned out. We've been robbed fifteen times. All of the jewelry, gone. A mink teddy bear, gone. The safe, emptied. When our own houses were robbed, Mom didn't lift a finger. She never tried to get anything back, even though she always knew exactly who did it. She didn't want to be a rat, and she felt sorry for the robbers. She figured if they were desperate enough to steal from a friend—and it's always a friend, because who else knows where the safe and valuables are?—they had to be in worse shape than she was. See what I mean? She's too forgiving!❞

—*Raquel, daughter*

NEVER COME BETWEEN A FRIEND AND HER BOYFRIEND

Never say one bad word about him. She might hate the guy's guts and be on the verge of breaking up. You might just be agreeing with her about what a jerk-off he is. But, if they make up the following week, you'll look like the bad guy who wanted them to end it. I stay neutral, reserve judgment. I feel weird telling people what to say or what to do in their romantic lives. It's not like my romantic history is so perfect! Unless you're in the relationship, you have no idea what's going on. Talk smack about a friend's boyfriend, and you might get smacked upside the head. No joke.

JUST LISTEN

Sometimes, the best thing you can do for a friend is shut up and listen. I'm good at that, from working in the bar business. Friends and customers alike tell me their sagas and ask my advice. As if I know anything! I'm not qualified to give anyone advice. They don't want it, anyway. People need to vent about their problems, so I let them, and I pay attention. I don't just nod along while thinking about dinner or what I'm going to wear later. People can tell, and they appreciate it. Whoever pours her heart out to me knows she's being heard.

STOP WITH THE CRYING

When a friend is upset, I'm always there to take her out for a drink or dinner and console her. If she's crying, I try to make her laugh, or just smile a little. Whenever I hang out with friends, depressed or not, I bring the fun and the drinks. It's called happy hour for a reason.

One guaranteed way to lift the spirits of a sad friend is to take her to a drag show. On *Mob Wives*, after Renee found out her ex-husband ratted out her father, she was a wreck. It was awful to witness. I felt so bad for her, so I got the girls together to take her to Lips, a drag-show club. Before long, she was laughing, singing. When she got up to dance with the drag queens, I knew my idea was a winner. The queens were hysterical. I love it when they talk in the low voices. Kind of sounds like my voice!

Attention trannies: if I go to a show and a drag Big Ang comes out, I will jump onstage and sing a duet of "You Don't Own Me" or "These Boots Are Made for Walkin'." Promise.

❝ The first time I got pregnant out of wedlock, I was scared and alone. Angela was there for me, helping out with my baby shower, baptism, at my apartment. When I got pregnant with my son twelve years later—not my smartest move—Angela made no judgment. She smiled and offered to help out again. I chose her to be his god-mother. For the baptism, she flew back from somewhere and came to church straight from the airport. With her hair in braids down to her humongous chest, with a dark tan, still smelling like sun lotion, she stood in front of the priest as he christened my son. It's a moment I'll never forget.

"Many years later, I was diagnosed with pancreatic cancer. It was six months of hell, torture, and tears for the people who loved me. At the hospital, I was given last rites three times. Obviously, I survived. I might not have if not for Angela's love and support. She held a benefit for me, raising money for my kids. Every time I opened my eyes at the hospital, she was at my bed, holding my hand or pet-ting my head. She was there at my first feeding after six months on an IV. When I finally went home, Angela threw a party for my fiftieth birthday to celebrate my life. And now, at her time to shine, she asked me to share the spot-light. I'm honored to tell the story, that I'm still here, in a large part, because she was there for me."

—Little Jenn, friend

THE HIT LIST

When Italians say *hit*, it's usually not good. To get a spot on the Hit List, people have to commit major infractions, like:

1. **INSULTING SOMEONE'S MOTHER.** Just unacceptable.

2. **TRASHING SOMEONE'S KIDS.** The worst. Whatever you say will come back to you, and Mama isn't going to be happy about it. We say, "If you spit in the air, expect to get splattered." Never is this more true than in bad-mouthing someone's kids.

3. **BLAMING ANOTHER MOTHER'S KIDS FOR SOMETHING YOUR KIDS DID.** If you point the finger of blame at someone else, it's like cursing yourself. Blaming is a form of ratting out, which is horrible enough. Not taking responsibility for your (and your kids') actions is being a rat *and* a chicken. Cowardice isn't as bad as disloyalty, but once you get that reputation, it's hard to live down.

4. **BACKSTABBING.** You don't like something I said or did? Then tell me. Women say, "I didn't say anything I wouldn't say to your face." Bullshit! How about this: don't say anything that you haven't *already* said to my face.

5. **JUDGING.** No one lives in anyone else's skin or lives her life. No one's perfect. So don't judge. Any judgment you make about another person will one day land at your door. Case in point: On *Mob Wives*, Renee judged Karen for her father's having been a rat. One year later, Renee's ex turned out to be a rat, and she had to face down harsh judgment.

What goes around *always* comes around.

❝ For the baby shower when Ang was pregnant with Raquel, I bought her a beautiful wrought-iron, round cradle. I tied it to the roof of my car and brought it to the shower in the city. Ang loved it and used it for Raquel and A.J. Then I pretty much forgot about it. And then, fifteen years later, my son, now eleven, was born after years and years of trying to get pregnant with in vitro. Ang had the round cradle repainted at a car store from white to cream, and she gave it back to me for my son. I was so touched. She'd kept it for me all these years, waiting for me to need it, and knowing I would someday.

"When we brought my son home in early December, Ang was at the house. It was her idea to put him in a Christmas stocking, to stuff the baby in there, and put him by the Christmas tree. We did it and took pictures. They were perfect for the holiday, and to announce the gift of our son. We made cards of the picture and sent it out to everyone announcing my angel sent from heaven. Ang always had these kinds of great, creative, visual ideas."

—*Sallyann, cousin*

YOU NEVER KNOW

One of my best friends for life can't be interviewed for this book.

I met Cari-Ann twenty years ago at a Brooklyn bar called the Log Cabin. She was working karaoke, and I was bartending. We instantly hit it off and started doing everything together. Scuba diving in Puerto Rico, clubbing in the city, parties, dinners. We even got plastic surgery together. I'd never clicked so well and quickly with a relatively new person. Hey, a twenty-year friendship in my world *is* new; I've known most of my girls for thirty, forty, fifty years. All my friends loved Cari-Ann, too, right from the start. Her creative, fun, and beautiful spirit was impossible to resist. She fit in perfectly.

Cari-Ann is the talented artist who painted the murals on the walls of the Drunken Monkey (one of my favorites: the chimp holding a roll of toilet paper on the wall across from the restrooms). She also did most of the tattoos on my body. One of my favorites: the bee on my left shoulder.

Why a bee? A bunch of our crew went on a breast-cancer walk in Prospect Park, Brooklyn, to support Cari-Ann. She'd been living with the disease for a few years by then. So we're out there, hoofing along, and I got stung by a bee. I had a bad reaction to the sting and had to be rushed to the hospital. It was scary, but also hilarious. We couldn't believe that, of all the people at this charity walk, a lot of them sick with cancer, I'm the one who's taken away in an ambulance. The bee is a reminder of that day.

When my grandson was born a few years ago, Cari-Ann came to bring him a baby gift. She was on her last legs, weak and completely bald, but she still managed to meet Sal. She fought the disease for five years and never lost hope. I was with her in the hospital when she died, and it was beautiful and terrible to witness. She was only forty-two. After she passed, I got a tattoo of a pink ribbon on my lower back. It's one of the only tattoos on my body that Cari-Ann didn't put there herself. It represents a pledge to honor her memory, and a vow to care for all of my friends, and to value them every day. You never know what can happen. One day, they could be gone.

“ A lot of people say they've got your back, but Ang really means it. We grew up next door to each other. My parents were always busy, so I spent a lot of time at Ang's house. There were seven kids there. What was one more? They took me everywhere with them. Even though I was ten years younger, Ang always included me, and she looked after me.

"Later on, I babysat Raquel and A.J. when Ang was still in Brooklyn. The kids were fun, and Ang always paid me very well. Too well! She knew my family didn't come from much money, and she made me the best-paid baby-sitter in Brooklyn. She was always generous, always drop-dead gorgeous in the most incredible outfits. She never bad-mouthed anyone. She was so sweet, no one could be jealous of her.

"Then she moved to Staten Island. We didn't see each other for about ten years. But when my sister died, Ang came right over as soon as she heard. She and Janine took over. We didn't have enough money to bury my sister, so Ang and Janine took care of it all. They made some calls to people they knew and helped us get an inexpensive funeral for my sister. I hadn't seen them in years, but they were right there, helping me and taking care of the logistics. I will never forget how wonderful they were."

—Lori, friend

FOLLOW THE DIAMOND RULE

You know the Golden Rule, right? Do unto others as you would have them do unto you? Well, I follow the diamond rule: Do unto others as you would have them do to your kids. Not that I treat my friends like children. It's that I feel responsible and protective of them, the same way I would my own flesh and blood. I care for them when they're sick, give them money when they're broke, and stand by them no matter what happens, for life. If you have that big a commitment to your friends, they'll always return the favor.

13
Big Men Rules

I had my first boyfriend at fifteen. He was the coolest kid in the neighborhood with the hottest car. But it didn't last. None of my relationships have lasted for long. Usually, it's because the guys cheat or screw up and I move on. Sometimes, it's because the guy drops dead. My family calls me the Black Widow. If you date me, you will have a heart attack or fall to a terrible disease or crash on your motorcycle. My husband, Neil, is aware of it. He's not afraid, though, either because he's delusional or because he has good health insurance. He says, "You're not going to lose me." And I look at all six feet seven inches of him and think, "He *is* easy to spot in a crowd."

If you're after wisdom about how to keep the home fires burning after forty years of marriage, you have come to the wrong place. But I do have some ideas about how to handle men while staying true to myself.

> " Herbie was a WWF wrestler and a former bouncer at Pastels. Ang and Jenn decided to take him out to dinner and go drinking with him. He was a massive man—four hundred pounds, easily. They wound up partying all night with this guy. Ang gets home and goes to bed. An hour later, we get a phone call. Herbie was dead. He had a heart attack, or something. That's why they call her the Black Widow. One night with her, this guy dropped dead."
>
> —Dominick, brother-in-law

> " When Ang was fifteen, she had a boyfriend. Someone told my mother that Ang ran away to marry him. The whole family went after them in the car and caught up to the couple in Virginia, where you can get married as young as fourteen, apparently. My parents made it in the nick of time and dragged Ang and the kid back to Brooklyn. That pretty much ended the relationship.
>
> "We looked him up recently on Facebook. He used to be really cute, but now ... I can see that he was never really her type. She dodged a bullet there."
>
> —Janine, sister

DON'T RELY ON A MAN TO SOLVE YOUR PROBLEMS

After my parents' divorce, I stayed at Dad's house. I was the only woman left there. Suddenly, I was expected to take on the role of mother and do all the cooking and washing. I went from being a teenage kid to a housewife. Didn't take long before I was sick of cleaning up after my brothers and father. I met a guy at a club—a tough mob guy—who was twice my age. He wanted to marry me. I wanted to get the hell out of Dad's house.

The marriage was a *nightmare*. It lasted less than a year. He was a bum. When I caught him cheating for the last time, I tried to burn his house down by setting the couch on fire. I took a match to it. The couch didn't go up in flames, though. It didn't exactly catch. I went through the whole book of matches one by one, no good. At worst, the cushion got singed. In hindsight, I should have lit them all at the same time, and I might've had better luck. Live and learn.

I packed my bags and sneaked out in the middle of the night, just like I used to do when I was a teenager. But this time, I snuck back to Mom's.

DON'T GO WACKO IN LOVE

I've had two great loves in my life (although neither lives up to my grandson). I can't go into detail about either of them. They have families, and out of respect, I'll stand by omertà. With one of them, he of the LOSAH tattoo, I had a wild, crazy, passionate affair that made me do foolish things—well, more foolish than usual. I was his girlfriend (he had a wife). We argued a lot. I think my hatred of fighting stems from this relationship, even more than listening to my parents. He was possessive and controlling, telling me where I could go, who I could see, what I could wear. No one was going to boss me around, especially not a married man. I pushed back, hard.

By the time our relationship ended, as brokenhearted as I was, I was also relieved. I didn't like feeling out of control emotionally. Generally, it makes people behave like assholes, and I do not want to be one of those. Now, with Neil, the main emotion I struggle with isn't mania. It's annoyance. If I go three days straight with a man, he starts to get on my nerves. I think marriage should be only every other night. That, I could live with.

" Ang got picked up by the cops because her boyfriend's wife accused her of phone harassment. She said Ang was calling her constantly and leaving threatening messages like 'He's mine. I got him, and you don't.' (Which may or may not have been true.) The cops took Ang in and went to fingerprint her, but because her nails were twelve feet long, they couldn't do it. So they got out these gardening shears and cut her nails off. The cops felt so bad about it that instead of putting her in a cell, they took us to lunch at the Saloon instead. In the end, the charges were dropped. Ang had to go to court three times, but the wife never showed up."

—Little Ang, friend

" Ang and Losah fought a lot. One time, Ang was dressed in Doc Martens boots, short shorts, a beautiful top, and full makeup to go to work at Nocturnals, her old bar. He got a load of her outfit—she looked gorgeous, but he thought it was too sexy. He said, 'This is how you dress for work?' And then they started fighting. Their relationship was tempestuous. Lots of fire—and ice. The next day after a fight, he'd come home with a Cartier bracelet or a ring to make up."

—Janine, sister

HOW TO CURE A BROKEN HEART

Get a new man, or a new dog.

Little Louie was my consolation prize after I threw Neil out the first time. Little Louie is cuter and smells better than any man, and when he pukes on the floor, it's just a neat little puddle and easy to clean up.

STICK WITH WHAT YOU KNOW

I always gravitated to the wiseguys. I've been with men from each of New York's Five Families. Jenn calls the roster of my exes "the Sixth Family." I've hung out in, bartended at, or owned mob hangouts since I was fifteen, so who else was I going to meet? I grew up around tough guys, so I feel most comfortable with them. Plus, they're exciting.

People laugh when I say this, but it's true: mob guys are handsome. Not all, but most. They carry themselves with a confidence, a swagger, that's hard to resist. When a mob guy walks into the room, he gives off the vibe that he's the Man, he's going to take care of you and make everything okay.

If they're not fat from too much home cooking, wise-guys stay in shape, with big guns. They go to the gym to get Dieseled. Throw in some sexy tattoos, and I melt. Okay, maybe that's not entirely true. He also has to be out of prison, taller than me, and have a lot of cash. Bonus points if he's not on crack, and if his mother is dead.

And wiseguys know how to tip! When I've worked at mob bars, on a busy night I could make thousands. Janine worked at the bar sometimes and, one night, made $2,000— at the coat check.

Even more important: wiseguys know shoes. I've never seen one who didn't appreciate quality footwear. Italian men love Italian leather. My husband, Neil, is Irish and wouldn't know a designer wing tip if I smashed him over the head with it. On his list of Most Important Things in life, Wearing Great Shoes falls somewhere below Visiting Kansas. He couldn't care less. I buy his shoes—size 12. Big man, big shoes, big all over. (Neil does not suffer from the Irish curse.) I recently bought him gorgeous red suede driving shoes that are so big Little Louie could sleep inside one.

John Gotti, to me, was the ideal man. He was the classiest guy I ever met. I knew him before he became the Dapper Don, although he always dressed well. I used to work at a Brooklyn mob bar called the Nineteenth Hole, and he'd come around. He was so handsome, I'd just stare at him. My celebrity crush is the actor who played Gotti in the movies: Armand Assante. I bet that man knows how to treat a woman, or three.

    ❝❝ As young kid, Angela was a hotshot. Great body, great smile, great person. She'd walk down the street and cars would just stop. Every man drooled over her, but she was innocent about it. She'd always be friendly without knowing the power that she had over them. That innocence still comes through now, despite all she's experienced. She's just a sweet, good-natured person."

—Deb, "aunt"

NO ONE OWNS ME

I've been described by some people as a mob girl, the companion of a gangster. Not the wife. Not the goomada (who is the official girlfriend). I'm the woman men hang out with, have fun with, and think of as one of the guys. The wife or a goomada has to settle down and devote herself to her man and be at his beck and call. I always preferred to be independent and put all the love and devotion other women put toward their husbands into raising my kids and having a good time. Besides my grand total of four years of married life (and counting), I've been my own woman. Actually, even when I am married, I'm independent. At my wedding three years ago, just to make this point loud and clear, our first dance was to Lesley Gore's "You Don't Own Me" (my theme song).

❝ I've known Ang for over thirty years, since we were nineteen and twenty. Ang was crazy back then. She would hop from bar to bar, always going out. She was a young kid looking for fun, like most twenty-year-olds—except she was in the VIP room at the club, hanging out with the old mob guys. She just happened to gravitate toward them and that type of atmosphere."

—*Dominick, brother-in-law*

TO GET A MAN'S ATTENTION, WHISPER

My voice is my trademark (along with my tits, lips, laugh, personality, and style; I guess I've got a lot of trademarks). My voice, aka the Voice, is deep as a foghorn. It's mainly due to a thyroid tumor that's wrapped around my vocal cords, plus a little acid reflux. Smoking brown cigarettes for forty years hasn't helped, either. Whatever the cause, guys tell me my low voice is sexy. I'm not as enamored with it as they are. I think it sounds like gravel soaking in Scotch. My friend Celia has the same voice. Her husband can't tell us apart on the phone, which we could take advantage of if the need ever arises. But seriously, ladies, if you use a lower register and drop your volume, a man will always lean in to hear you better.

OLDER MEN ARE SEXY

Dad was twenty years older than Mom. Maybe that's why I never saw anything strange about dating much older men. The benefit of dating geezers: they've got bank. The drawback: they'll probably die soon. Or maybe that's just another benefit.

Jenn and I were at the Ponte Vecchio, a mob hangout in Brooklyn, not *too* long ago, sitting at the bar. I pointed out a guy I'd dated back in the day and said, "He's hot."

She practically spit out her drink. "That guy? He's like a hundred years old!"

Okay, his skin might've looked like cracked Corinthian leather left out in the sun. His hair might've looked like a diseased squirrel crawled on top of his head to take a nap. And he walked with a cane, had a hearing aid, and his old-man ass was dragging on the floor. What*ever*. When I went out with him twenty years ago, he was the toughest guy in town. I remembered him fondly—he bought me a fur coat.

  ❝ During her late twenties and thirties, Ang had dating binges. She'd go out with a lot of older wiseguys, including a lot of my father's friends. She loved them, and, man, did they love her. Always have. When we were fifteen and sixteen, we started going out to clubs. And she'd always head right over to the older crew. I had to be careful, though. My dad, Sally Lombardi, didn't allow me to go to those places. If anyone heard my name, I wouldn't be let in. Whenever I was with Ang, I'd say I was her cousin Barbara. Dad could bar me from the clubs, but he couldn't bar her. We'd get in and would be having a good time. Angela would get wacked and say, 'Hey, she ain't my cousin Barbara. She's Sallyann!' She thought it was hilarious. And then we'd get thrown out."

—*Sallyann, cousin*

YOUNGER MEN ARE TROUBLE

The main reason to date younger guys: They live longer. They don't have wrinkles on their liver spots. Their balls aren't tucked into their socks. The drawbacks: they're often broke, drunk, more likely to cheat, lie, or steal.

Neil is the first much younger guy I've been with—he's only thirty-nine. He lived up to the erratic stereotype—at first. Things are better now. I'm keeping a close eye on him.

WHEN A MAN OFFERS YOU A GIFT, TAKE IT

If the man I'm with wants to lavish me with gifts, I'm not going to insult him by saying no. Mob guys are generous. They shower women with presents. Over the years, they've bought me beautiful furs, diamonds, cars, my precious Persian cats. One guy bought me houses (at one time I owned four). If we were driving around and I said, "Oooh, I love that house," he'd pull into the driveway, walk up to the front door, ring the bell, and ask the owner, "Can I buy your house for my girlfriend?" Sometimes, the owners would do it. We once staked out a house for a year—a gorgeous bungalow on the beach—until the owner said, "Okay, you want it so bad, you can have it."

One particular boyfriend, Mister X, really knew how to

spoil a woman. He had a wife and a goomada, so, on the books, I was his number three. But he treated me like number one. He said, "Every day is your birthday!" He'd hand me jewelry and designer clothes wrapped in boxes. My sister and brother-in-law figured out that, in one year, Mister X spent about $3 million on me (including a $1.2 million house). He was the kindest, most generous man. Sadly, several years ago, Mister X died. My brother-in-law, in his room, still has a picture of him, and when Dom looks at it, he says, "Man, I really miss that guy." Even after we broke up, he stayed in touch with Janine and Dom.

I took it all, no hesitation, and said, "Thank you." But it was always understood that, although they bought me things, the men never owned me. They never even rented me. It was a close friendship with benefits. They benefited from my company. And I benefited from their generosity.

" Ang and Mister X went to the track in Saratoga and won fifty thousand dollars betting on horses. On the ride home, she would fling her long Rasta braids over his head while he was driving. Kind of dangerous—but exciting. Mister X cracked up every time. He kept saying, 'This is why I love her.' "

—Janine, sister

DON'T FALL IN LOVE SO HARD YOU CAN'T GET UP

Unlike some of my friends who get their heart broken every time, I don't get emotionally attached. The guys do. I've never loved a man more than he loved me. You might say, "How can you control your emotions and keep them in check?" When you've had as many relationships as I have, you don't fall for anything, including head over heels in love.

ALWAYS WAKE UP IN YOUR OWN BED

When I'm with a guy, no matter how late (or early) it is, no matter how tired I am, or how comfortable, I get out of bed and go home. I'm fine with men sleeping over at my place (especially if he bought the place), but I won't stay at theirs. Without fail, I'd get home by 7:00 a.m. to be there when my kids wake up. Whenever men complained about my leaving in the middle of night, I just explained that I don't like sleeping out of my house. Now that I think about it, maybe that's why they bought me houses.

NO SLOPPY SECONDS—
OR THIRDS

Why on earth would you want to be with a guy your friend has already had? Just off the bat, there's something wrong with a woman who chases her friends' exes. She's got something to prove. I have no clue what that might be, though, because I don't take sloppy seconds.

No matter how handsome or rich a man might be, if he's been with one of my friends, he is off-limits. I don't care if he was with the friend ten years ago, or twenty years ago. If she says she doesn't care who he gets in bed with, it doesn't matter. She might even believe it to the bottom of her heart. But if her pal got with the guy, and she found out—even if she hasn't thought about him in years—she'll feel betrayed, which will turn into anger. And, guaranteed, she won't be pissed off at the guy for putting his dick where it doesn't belong. She'll be furious with her girlfriend.

Men think they're the territorial ones. But women are much worse. Once a woman has been naked with someone, it's like she's put her mark on him. No matter how many other women he sleeps with, has kids with, or marries after her, in her head, she has a claim. I'm not saying it makes any sense. But I've seen friendships explode over some guy neither woman cared about or even liked.

On the other side, the one who got there second (or

hundredth) will always wonder, did he like her more? Did he think she was sexier? Imagining your friend with your boyfriend, being intimate? That's not a good picture for a new relationship. Plus, there's always the danger that, once this guy is brought back into your social circle, he'll want to have sex with his ex again. Men (and some women) believe that if they've been with someone before—even years before—and they do it again, it's not cheating. Wrong. But it does happen.

DON'T PUT OUT ON THE FIRST DATE

If a woman has sex on the first date, I guarantee that man will never buy her a house. Should she ever see him again, it'll be by accident, like at the gas station or the local bar, and it will be weird.

If a woman has sex on the second date, that man will never buy her a car. He might treat her to dinner at the Greek diner or Wendy's, but more likely, he'll just call her a cab.

If a woman waits until the third or fourth date, the man *might*, one day, buy her diamond jewelry (no bets on a ring). He will definitely take her out to a decent restaurant. It's possible that, down the road, he'll want a monogamous relationship.

In which case, I have one word: *Runforyourfreakin'life!*

I never have sex with a guy until I've known him for *months*. On the first ten dates, I say, "Pick me up in a nice car. Take me to the best restaurant. I'll order the most expensive food and the finest wine. Then you can pay for it, take me home, and drive away. 'Bye!"

The longer you wait, the more generous he'll be. That is true, but it's not why I hold them off. I do it so we'll like each other better. As soon as you add sex, the situation changes. So do the people involved. The woman you were before you had sex is not who you'll be the morning after.

The longer you wait before you do it, though, the better chance you have, as an individual and a couple (God help you), to get to know and like the other person and figure out whether he's worth (1) your time, and (2) the aggravation.

YOU CHEAT, I LEAVE

I have zero tolerance for men who cheat. None. If I find out my boyfriend (or husband) has been with another woman, I end the relationship. One strike, and he's *out*.

Some women look the other way and wait for the guilt gifts to come in. Although I love furs and jewels as much as anyone, there aren't enough diamonds in all of South Africa to buy me off if my man has cheated. In that case, I don't want gifts. I want revenge.

The revenge fuck: I've done it. I have some rules, though. I won't do it with my boyfriend's brothers, cousins, or close friends. That's like peeing in your own swimming pool. Even if I never want to see the cheating bastard again, sleeping with someone close to him—a person I might already be friends with—can hurt too many people and damage innocent bystanders.

I can sniff out a cheater in one deep inhale. It's obvious. I don't even have to go looking for it. A guy with a piece on the side thinks with his dick—and, no matter how big it is, it ain't too smart! I know all the tricks. On their cell phone, they use a man's name instead of their girlfriend's (Paul for Paulette, or Don for Donna). He spends less time with his kids, and more time at the gym. He calls to say he's working late—for the third night in a row—but doesn't answer the work phone. He says he's with a friend, but this friend just so happens to be sitting in front of me at the bar. He comes home in the morning and says, with a straight face, "I honestly don't know where I spent the night." Yeah? Well, *I've* got a pretty good idea!

DON'T MARRY FOR LOVE. MARRY FOR A PENSION

I didn't marry any of my boyfriends (although a lot of them would have loved to). It wasn't until I was forty-nine—thirty years after my first divorce—that I got stupid again and married Neil.

He was different from the get-go. All my life, I'd dated older, Italian wiseguys with lots of money to burn, no steady "job," big, loud families, and a bid (or two) in prison behind them, and, most likely, another on the horizon.

Neil is younger (by twelve years), Irish, from a middle-class upbringing, a sanitation worker on the city payroll with health insurance and a pension. He comes from a small, quiet family and has no connection to the Lifestyle at all. He's never been in prison, not even to visit relatives. I'm telling you, bringing him into my life was like beaming an alien to Planet Pasta down from Mars.

Neil grew up down the street from the Drunken Monkey and came into the bar a lot. We started talking, and then he asked me out. We had lunch a few times and got friendly, exchanged numbers. Slowly, we started calling each other and going out. It was a year and a half between our first lunch and our first night. A few weeks after that, we moved in together.

My family wasn't sure about him. Neil was so quiet

compared to us. Anyone who didn't speak up was suspect. They said, "He's just there. He's in a coma even when he's wide-awake!"

Janine always defended him: "He has a good heart."

That may be, but Neil wasn't one of us. That was obvious. It didn't matter so much to me. We got along well. Neil was reliable. I needed health insurance. I liked having a man in my life, and I was sick of watching them go to prison. So we got married.

But as I learned fast enough, the surface differences don't mean shit. I thought, "I'll marry a guy who's not going to disappear on the lam, or into solitary confinement, and see how that goes. I'll play it safe." And what happens? Turns out, a man is a man is a man. Irish, Italian, wiseguy, city worker, it doesn't matter.

They're all bums.

  " Our marriage hasn't been easy. For half of it, we were separated. She's kicked me out a few times. She doesn't take any shit and threw my stuff on the front lawn. She had the locks changed several times.

"It was a hundred percent my fault. I was a bar guy. I had some trouble finding my way home when I was drinking. I got some intervention, and now I don't drink at all.

Our fights were always about my drinking. Since I stopped, we don't fight. We're trying again with our marriage, and I hope it works out this time. Ang is a good wife and she deserves a good husband. She cooks and cleans and takes care of me. She puts clothes out for me, because you can't dress badly when you're with Big Ang. The age difference doesn't bother me. She doesn't act even close to fifty-two. Flip it. She acts like she's twenty-five.

"Ang would give you the shirt off her back, but she doesn't say how she feels. I'd like to get an 'I love you' out of her. I'd take an 'I like you.' But even if I don't hear it, I have to assume she likes having me around. She took me back three times. She's not very romantic or affection-ate (unless she's wacked). That's not her style. She doesn't hold hands, or kiss and hug in front of people. We rarely go on romantic date nights, or even have a night alone at home. I go to sleep with her family and friends in the house, and I wake up with them here. No such thing as a quiet night, chilling in front of the TV. But it's okay. I'm getting used to it. If you're with Ang, you're at the center of the action."

—Neil, husband

AFTER YOU THROW THE BUM OUT, YOU CAN LET HIM BACK IN

Usually, my rule is (short of cheating) "Three strikes and he's *out*." Neil is on his fourth strike. What can I say? Neil got treatment. I wanted him to get sober, and he did. I took him back in. We take it one day at a time. I haven't completely forgiven him, though, and I don't trust him 100 percent yet. But I'm giving him a chance. Twenty years ago, he'd be long gone. I'd be brushing off my hands and saying, "Next!"

I must be getting soft in my old age.

THE MOST IMPORTANT RULE ABOUT MARRIAGE IS . . .

Don't let him eat in bed.

Neil is a sanitation worker and puts in long, hard twelve-hour days. He comes home hungry and tired. I can't fault him for that. But I *can* give him shit when he gets in bed with a mortadella sandwich, then falls asleep with the half-eaten hero in his hand! I woke up with a piece of mortadella stuck to my leg and sesame seeds from the bread dotted all over me like I'd been rolled in them. I looked over at him, and he was sound asleep with crumbs on his chin and sausage in his hair.

Idiot.

It's like having another child. I'm constantly picking up after him. Cleaning his dishes, putting his dirty clothes in the wash. But sleeping with a sandwich took his slob tendencies to a new level. I can't speak for everyone, but I do not want to peel a greasy slab of meat off my leg first thing in the morning!

14
Big Pet Rules

*I*f you're not an "animal person," don't come to my house. I won't lock my dogs in a room or shoo my cats off the furniture. I've always shared my life with pets. I treasure my purebreds, but I've got an especially soft spot for strays. I can't imagine coming home and not being greeted at the door by some furry creature. And I don't mean my husband.

❝ We had a poodle named Tiny, a Yorkie named Tiger. A golden, a sheepdog—can't remember their names. Ang had a chow named Chin and took him with her when she got married the first time. But the dog jumped out the window and ran back home to Mom's house—like Ang did, not too long after. We always had plenty of cats, too, and a parakeet.

"What was a big mystery growing up was how, whenever my parents brought home a new baby, all the pets would disappear. We found out years later it was because my dad rounded them up and took them to the creek. He tried to get rid of them, but they'd come back, or we'd get more."

—*Ronald, brother*

WATCH OUT FOR PUDDLES

My Pomeranian Little Louie might pee on your shoes and poop on the floor (hey, he gets excited and shit happens). Yeah, it's not cute. I have to clean up after him all the time. But he's just a dog. Dogs mark their territory. When Louie pees on the floor or your leg, he's saying, "This is mine." Since I got him a few months ago, Louie has put his mark on me, every room of my house, and all my friends and family, many times. For a little dog, his territory includes half of Staten Island! But it's nice to know he counts us as his own.

B·I

66 I have two pit bulls. Missy, the brown one, and Kilo, who's blind. I'm bringing Kilo to move back in with Mom, but I have to leave Missy with my dad. She's a mental patient—but smart. She can open the fridge door, ransack the food, and then close the door. You open the door, look in the fridge, and it's like a bomb went off. She's spiteful, too, and has a problem with little dogs. If I brought her to the new place, Missy would eat Little Louie in one bite.

"But Kilo is coming with me. She's special. I adopted her as a newborn. When I was fourteen, I was out on Halloween and saw a guy walking by with a brand-new puppy. He told me where the rest were, and there was Kilo. I had to have him. He was the first dog I brought home, just showed up with a blind, sick, premature puppy. Mom took one look at him and fell in love. Kilo was so cute, she couldn't deny him. He has bad allergy and skin problems, though, and needs a lot of care. Mom always helps with the vet and medicine bills. She once drove two hours to New Jersey to see a specialist for Kilo's skin condition. Anything under Mom's care will get the best."

—A. J., son

SPOIL THE PETS

It's a horror that my dad tried to ditch our pets! I'm probably still making up for his bad behavior by spoiling my pets now.

Louie was named after Louis Vuitton. Like my Louis Vuitton purse, he goes where I go. I can tuck him under my arm and carry him like a football (he weighs less than one). Or he's got a rhinestone-studded leash, his favorite accessory. He has a full closet, including a leather bomber jacket, a hoodie, a shiny orange parka. My favorite for summer: his baby-blue, sparkly sneakers, numbered one through four, with matching baby-blue socks and a onesie with his name on it. It was made by Simply Pets, only available at Country Mouse, my sister Janine's store on Forest Avenue. I get most of his clothes at the Hollywood Puppy Shop. We don't wear matching outfits for our walks because that would be a bit much (which is saying a lot, coming from me). But we always turn heads at the dog run.

I spoil him with attention, too. If he feels ignored (which he does about ten seconds after I put him down), he barks for attention in cute little yips. If I'm sitting down, he puts his tiny front paws on my knees to get me to put him on my lap, which would be annoying if he weren't so freakin' cute. (He's too small to jump up on my lap. He can't even make it onto the couch.) Yeah, Louie's a greedy beggar for affection, and he loves resting his head on my boobs.

Who wouldn't?

I also have two cats. Gigi and Georgie are twin Persians, a gift from an ex-boyfriend. The girls are fluffy. They have a tight grooming schedule (like their mama) and get their fur washed and cut every few months. They get their nails done. Sometimes, I pay extra for them to get little kitty massages when they're being groomed. Hey, they have a rough life of eating, sleeping, and being adored all day. They need their pampering time, too.

" One of the cats went missing a couple of years ago. I don't know which—they're twins and I can't tell them apart. A neighbor saw the cat on the street and called a service to come get it. I have no idea why she didn't call us, but whatever. The animal service people came, caught the cat, and took it away. After a million phone calls, we found out that the cat was taken to an animal shelter in Pennsylvania. The second we got the info, Ang was running out the door to the car. She dropped everything to drive two hours to this shelter to pick up the cat, and two hours back. I joked around and said, 'Why not just leave her there? The pussy's not worth it.' Yeah, that joke didn't go over too well. Ang is serious about her pets. They really are like children. And, in this house, no cat gets left behind."

—Neil, husband

DOGS AND CATS ARE
NEVER RATS

Unconditional love. That's what my pets give me, which is a lot more than I could possibly give them. Also, they don't talk. No matter what they see or hear, I know it'll never come back to me.

15

Big Party Rules

*P*arties are the easiest and most fun way to maintain relationships. Just have all your family and friends get their asses over to your house. To plan a great party, all I need are three things: (1) a reason, (2) a location, and (3) plenty of booze. Bada bing, I'm having a bash. I don't care if the reason to have a party is as flimsy as wet toilet paper (which reminds me: for a party, I always buy extra TP, paper towels, garbage bags, and cups, cups, cups). Give the people any excuse to kick back, they will flock to wherever I ask them to. And I am the best host. I always serve great drinks, food, play the best music (classic disco is a sure winner). Goes without saying, I dress festively. If they're coming out to see me, I want them to say, "It was worth it just to see what Ang was wearing." And of course I have to shop for something nice and sexy. I don't want to disappoint my guests.

“ Any excuse to throw a party. Mom will have people over—twenty, thirty people—for any holiday. The whole family arrives, and Mom makes sure everyone is eating and drinking and feels comfortable. If she sees someone sitting by themselves, Mom goes over to talk or brings the person into the conversation. She takes such good care of her guests, no one ever wants to leave. Her parties can go on for days.

“For my eighteenth birthday, my girlfriend and Mom threw a surprise party for me at our house on Drake Avenue. My girlfriend and I went out to eat, and then she said she didn't want to go out after. We went back home and—surprise. All my friends. A mountain of food. We were only gone for an hour or two. Mom can move real fast when she wants to.”

—A.J., son

FIRST SNOW PARTY

Every winter when the first flake falls from the sky, we throw a First Snow Party. One year, we did it at Fortune Garden, and it was the craziest storm of the century. It just kept coming down—two, three feet of snow. People blew in like snowmen, just covered head to toe. We wound up getting snowed in at the restaurant and partied all night long, as the piles got higher and higher on the street outside. When it finally stopped snowing, our cars were buried. My friends will, literally, drive through a blizzard to get to one of my parties.

I once had a First Snow Party at the house on the beach, and the whole family got snowed in. After two days, the guys got stir-crazy. A.J., John, and Louis got on quads and went to the store for more supplies. When they made it back, the party kept going.

❝ Ang and I, along with a couple of friends and my then-four-month-old daughter, were on the beach in Coney Island. We saw a cigarette boat go by. Ang said, 'Look, Aunt Deb, there's my friend in the boat. Let's go.' She flagged him down.

"I said, 'What about the baby?'

"One of my friends said, 'I'll take her. You go, have fun.'

"So Ang and I got on the boat, and her friend took us to Mill Basin to a party on a yacht. Dancing, drinking, Jacuzzis. Gorgeous men and women everywhere. And then, two hours later, he brought us back to Coney Island. This was a normal, everyday adventure for Ang. But I was married with a little baby, and my life was feeling kind of boring. But when you're with Ang, life gets exciting on a moment's notice.

"That was true thirty years ago, and it's still true. When she came to Florida last time, I took her to a casino. I like to shoot craps, but I don't win. With Ang, though, we won eight hundred dollars. She was my good-luck charm, cheering me on and getting everyone around to join in. No one can resist her."

—Deb, "aunt"

ANYTHING GOES

It's not a party unless there's mass chaos. I want people running around the house, jumping in the pool, throwing up in the bushes. I want hookups and wild dancing, people calling me the next day, saying, "It was out of control!" or "I cannot believe what happened last night."

When I throw a party, I go all out, no holds barred. I want to make jaws drop. For birthday parties, I get the huge blow-up bouncy castles for the kids. For weddings, how about an ice sculpture of a swan with vodka streaming out of its beak? A tattoo artist for spontaneous inking? Done. For my fiftieth, and for a couple of Fourth of Julys (and my wedding), I hosted a White Party. Everyone came dressed head to toe in white. My crew usually wears a lot of black, colors, and prints. White isn't our usual style. I don't think anything that started pure white at the beginning of the party looked that pristine at the end.

> ❝ The party doesn't start until Ang shows up. I remember when we were going on a dinner cruise for Margo's fiftieth birthday, we had to take a bus to the city to get to the ship. No one was happy about the long bus ride, despite the champagne. Then Ang arrives at the bus with a life preserver around her waist that she'd pulled off the wall at a tavern the night before. She couldn't fit down the bus aisle and was bumping into all the seats. And then she started passing out swimmies—those little arm floats kids wear—saying, 'Only one swimmie per person. Lots of luck if you fall overboard!' We all died laughing. The mood shifted, and the bus ride was suddenly rocking. We got to the dock in the city and climbed off the bus. I turned around, and the cruise crew was pushing Ang in a luggage cart toward the boat. We laughed all night long."
>
> —Denise, friend

WHITE WEDDING

Who says only the bride can wear white? When Neil and I got married, we did a whole white wedding. Neil and A.J. wore matching white linen suits with white Gucci sandals. Sal was in a tiny white suit and was pulled down the aisle in a little wagon. My niece was the flower girl, she looked like a little angel.

My dress? I wore a white satin, halter-top, backless, ankle-length gown that was an absolute show—and heart—stopper. I had a savage dark tan, which looked fab against the shiny fabric of the dress. My hair was blown stick straight and was so black it was practically blue. Diamonds on my wrists, neck, and ears. I felt pretty as fuck.

I might not exercise much, but I can haul ass when I need to. I can move houses in three days and plan a party in four. When Neil and I decided to get married, we set the wedding date for one month later. Two hundred and twenty people showed up at 2:00 p.m. at Janine's house for the wedding in the backyard around the pool. The guests didn't leave until 2:00 a.m. the next day. People fell down the steps. They passed out in the bushes. A guy walked in with a cane and left in a wheelchair. It was a twelve-hour marathon of eating, drinking, and mayhem. Neil reminds me that, in keeping with the white theme, we went through ten cases of chardonnay, and twenty-two half-gallon bottles of vodka.

Jenn had the top piece of the cake custom-made. The bride was made out of a Dom Pérignon bottle, and the groom was a Coors Light can. And that said it all.

" Ang's White Party at my restaurant was a blast. It was outdoors, right on the water. Everyone was dressed in white, and a lot of them were drinking tequila. One guy there, he thought he was John Travolta in a white suit. Anyway, someone went up to him, complimenting his outfit. She had high heels on that were too high for walking around on grass, and she tripped and spilled red wine all over him. The guy didn't think it was so funny. But Ang said, "You know, it looks better with the splash of red." I had this green spray paint for dry patches in the grass. We got the idea to spray his white shoes green and said, "Now you'll really stand out." He looked great! Red, white, and green, the colors of the Italian flag. He didn't think it was so funny, but we though it was hysterical."

—Angelina, friend

NO CONFLICTS

If two party invites come for the same night, I leave town. That's one way to avoid the tension over a scheduling conflict. Or, if I have to stick around, I make the tough choice and go to the better friend's party. Since all my best friends would be at the same gathering, it's unlikely I'd have to choose between equals.

KNOW WHEN TO SAY WHEN

The short answer: if you're not driving, there is no "when."
I'm not saying you should drink until you pass out cold (at
least not every freakin' night!). But if you're in a good place
among friends, and you don't have anywhere in particular to
be (like a job or back home with your spouse and kids), then
why not enjoy yourself, have a few drinks, and get wacked?
The only consequences are making a fool of yourself, falling
down, breaking bones or the furniture, and a brain-crippling
hangover. My advice: go to the hospital for broken bones,
and go to Fortune Garden for the aching head. Or maybe skip
the hospital and just go to Fortune Garden, but I don't think
sticking a busted arm in a bowl of wonton soup will help.
(Then again, what do I know? I'm not a doctor.)

" Hanging out with Ang is always a riot. We went to Atlantic
City fifteen years ago. I'd just gotten separated from my
ex-husband and needed cheering up. We were drinking at
a club. Ang could drink and drink. After five hours, I quit.
She kept going. She was standing straight up one second,
and then she started to pitch forward, passing out. She fell
over and landed at a tilt, like a seesaw. Her boobs were so
big, she landed on a slant! I'll never forget it."

—Renee, Mob Wives castmate

HOW TO CURE A HANGOVER

Have another drink.

ALWAYS HAVE HOT GUYS AROUND

It's not a party without sexy men. I need some Dieseled guys to dance with (and to move the furniture around). Gay, straight, strangers, friends, cousins, whatever. Just show up, and take your shirt off.

DON'T WAIT TO CELEBRATE

Holding off on throwing a party for some event or holiday? Hey, it's Thursday. That's good enough. You won't go to the grave wishing you'd partied less. So make any night special. Make *every* night special. Or your life will go by, while you're waiting to make plans.

16

Big Bar Rules

Both my parents were bartenders, and I've taken up the family trade. I've been mixing drinks for longer than I can remember. I'm not a barfly, I'm a bar butterfly—I flit around in colorful clothes, going from group to group, and making everyone happy. If relationships don't unfold around the kitchen table, they do at the local watering hole. Other than my house, bars are where I feel most at home.

HIRE PEOPLE YOU CAN TRUST

I always employ my family. At the Drunken Monkey, everyone who works there is either family or like family. My daughter works behind the bar at night. My husband and nephew help out. My best friend, Margo, takes the day shifts. I run the place with Sallyann, my cousin. If I need extra help on a busy night, I pick up the phone and enlist a sister, brother, or friend, basically whoever answers and has a few hours to spare.

The good thing about only working with family is that I don't have to go through an uncomfortable interviewing process to hire people. I can only imagine the degenerates who'd apply to work at the Drunken Monkey (I'm rolling my eyes at the thought). If something goes wrong at the bar, I can say to Neil, "You didn't get more marshmallow-flavored vodka, and now we're out! What's the matter with you?" And it's fine. It's expected. Comfortable. It's like being at home in the kitchen. I'd hate to have to talk like a boss lady to someone who wasn't family. Even if someone sucks at bartending or steals, I can't bring myself to fire him. Someone else has to do it.

❝ The reason I wanted to go into business with Ang is because she's fabulous. She's been working in bars since she was fifteen, she knows everyone and could bring in a lot of customers. The Drunken Monkey came about because we needed a place for people in our age group to go. Ang and I are both independent types. We really wanted to run our own bar and stop working for other people. And now, we are."

—Sallyann, cousin

IT'S PERSONAL *AND* BUSINESS

When someone crosses me and then refuses to admit she was wrong, I can forgive, but it's hard to forget. I don't carry around the grudge, but I will let go of the friendship. Life's too short. I'm too busy for bullshit, or false friends.

Recently, my bar was robbed by a couple of morons. We'd remodeled the Drunken Monkey and took out the kitchen to make more room for customers and live music. We loaded the fridge, a sink, and some other valuable stuff into a big trailer. It was parked right in front of the bar. On a Sunday morning around 3:00 a.m. when the bar was still packed, two idiots from the neighborhood tried to drive away with the trailer. Sallyann was standing right outside the bar smoking and saw the whole thing. She got Dominick and Jimmy the bouncer to go after them. The thieves ditched the trailer and were caught by highway cops like twenty minutes later.

I knew one of the morons. He was the boyfriend of the daughter of a friend of mine. When I told the friend what happened, she defended him, even though he'd tried to rob me and was caught red-handed. If it were my daughter, I would be trying to get her away from this idiot. But my friend made excuses for him. We had a tense conversation—not a fight. Just a discussion. She's not coming around my bar anymore, and I'm glad.

No matter how forgiving you are, sometimes you have to draw the line. If she comes to me later and apologizes, I'm sure I'll get over it. But, meanwhile, she made her choice and now she can live with it.

> 66 We've definitely disagreed about some people. Ang would say someone was okay, and I'd say, 'Stay away from this one. She'll stab you in the back.' This one woman, J., came to the bar and seemed suspicious to me. She went out the back door, where she wasn't supposed to go. The door hit her, and she got hurt. She sued us and our landlord.
>
> "We almost lost the bar—and our homes—because of her. Eventually, she took us to court—and lost. We didn't see her for years, and then, unbelievably, she started coming around again. She was nuts! Margo and I were like 'What is she doing here?' But Ang accepted her back in."
>
> —Sallyann, cousin

IF YOU SMOKE IN MY BAR, YOU BETTER BE ON FIRE

I smoke More 120s. They're long, thin, and brown, closer to cigarillos than cigarettes. I have to special-order them by the carton because you can't find them in regular stores. I know it's bad for me, and I think about quitting. I just haven't managed to do it yet. It's one thing to smoke my own cigarettes, but I don't want to smoke fifty other people's, too. I agree with NYC mayor Bloomberg's law that bans smoking in bars. So, if you come to the Drunken Monkey and light up, you will get hosed. Take that shit outside. That's why we have a bench out there, and it's always crowded, so you won't feel lonely.

"We heard that a church all the way uptown on 125th Street was closing, and they were auctioning off all the old stuff. So Ang and I went to check it out. We saw these incredible Gothic, red-glass light fixtures on long chains and thought they'd be perfect for the Drunken Monkey. Ang decided we *had* to buy them, so did. We paid next to nothing for a dozen of these huge lights.

The only problem was, we had driven Angela's little Jag convertible. We put them in the tiny space behind the seat, and I held them down as we drove back to Staten Island. We're racing down the highway. I'm holding on. The chains are dragging on the road. The fixtures were almost falling off the back of the car. Eventually, the cops started following us. With Ang, no matter how terrifying things are, they're also funny. We finally got the fixtures back to the bar and hung them. She was right. They're perfect. And now, whenever I look up at them, I picture us in that tiny car, speeding down the highway, and crack up."

—*Margo, friend and bartender at the Drunken Monkey*

LOVE MY GAYS

And my gays love me. For years, I've hosted Gay Night at my bars. A lot of times, it's just the gay bartender, the gay DJ, and me. My best friend, Cari-Ann, who was a lesbian, did all the monkey mural paintings on the walls. I feel like her spirit lives permanently in the bar because of her art. (You might be wondering, "What's up with the freakin' monkeys?" I just love them. I want one for a pet so bad. I've always wanted one. Instead, I have a dozen on my bar walls, and monkey art all over my house.)

I don't care why the gays love me, just as long as they do! And I love them right back. When I do events at gay bars in the city, I have the best time. So many handsome men there. (Shout-out to Splash on West Seventeenth Street: the most gorgeous bartenders in Manhattan!) I try not to disappoint them—or any customers who come to the bar—so I always dress nice and show off the boobs. Why gay men get such a kick out of my boobs is a mystery to me. The lesbians love them, too, but that makes more sense.

> 66 The gays love her so much because she looks like a big transvestite on TV. She's tall, with a deep voice, and the big boobs, big lips. The lighting and makeup make her look like a man in drag. But when they come to meet her at the bar, they realize that's not the case. She's very feminine and pretty in real life."
>
> *—Margo, friend and bartender at the Drunken Monkey*

OH, JUST DRINK IT!

When I pour a shot for a customer at the bar, I get annoyed if she doesn't drink it right away. You're in a bar, for Christ's sake. Do the shot. One, two, three, down!

> 66 One time at the Drunken Monkey, some drunk guy sat at the bar next to me and A.J. He said, 'Hey, did you see the bartender with the big boobs?' A.J. just gave me a look. I knew he was furious.
>
> "I said, 'I don't know who you're talking about and shut the fuck up.'
>
> "I got A.J. away from him and calmed him down. I think I stopped him from killing someone that night."
>
> *—Kevin, A.J.'s best friend*

NASTY DRUNKS

Want to have a great time, meet some people, relax, dance, sing karaoke, make out, chat with old friends and new? You will always be welcomed in my bar. I will mix drinks for you, pose for pictures, whatever you want. But if you're a drunk, nasty asshole, and you're obnoxious to my other customers, bark at people (it happens), hit aggressively on women (or men), put your hands on anyone who does not appreciate it, then you are not welcome. My bouncers will pick you up by the nut sack and throw you out on the street. And when your sorry rat ass lands on the pavement, I'll smile.

And then, I'll take pity on you. If I liked you before you turned into a drunken asshole, I might drive you home. If I think you might puke or stink up my Jag, I'll call you a cab. I might even wind up paying for it.

I forgive everyone—way too easily and quickly. That's how stupid I am. I've never banned someone for life from my bars. If you come in the next night and apologize, I'll forget the ugly ever happened.

Cross me again? You better watch out or I might . . . oh, who am I kidding? I'll probably let you off again. But don't get too comfortable on that stool. My family members, those working and those hanging out at the bar, aren't nearly as forgiving as I am.

DO NOT DRIVE DRUNK

This is an absolute, nonnegotiable. I've left my car all over the five boroughs and taken cabs home. I've had friends pick me up all over the city. No one leaves my bar wacked with keys in his hand.

LOSAHS WELCOME

When someone comes into the bar moping and complaining about whatever went wrong that day, I point at his face and yell, "Losah!" Then, I pour him a shot. I don't mean the guy is actually a loser (although he might be). The truth is, we all have days that make us feel like losers (my number one bad day: getting arrested). Rather than wallow in the saga, it's better to laugh it off, call yourself the biggest sorry-ass, pathetic LOSAH in the world, have a shot, and *get over it*. Three minutes later, your day won't feel as much like a freakin' horror.

SPEAK THE FUCK UP

It's no wonder my voice is so low. Besides the health reasons, it's also been affected by my yelling at people from behind a crowded bar for decades. You know how many times I have to raise my voice to say, "What can I get you? What? *WHAT??*" to customers every night? Decades of screaming over loud, thumping music until 4:00 a.m. have taken their toll. (My hearing? Don't even get me started. I can't hear anything!) Someone should print up flash cards that say, "Vodka tonic, please!" and "Long Island Iced Tea here!"

I don't know if it's because of my low tone, but I do notice that, when I open my mouth, people tend to shut up and listen. Not only that, but they lean in to hear. They hang on my words. Otherwise, they might not understand what the hell I'm trying to say. I don't think that my words are any more or less fascinating than other people's. It's just that, when I say them, the sound is interesting, which makes the words themselves seem to have gravity. Try it: Go up to your husband and say in a loud, nagging, squeaky voice, "Take out the garbage." The next night, do it with a low, sexy whisper. He might not take out the trash no matter how you say it. But he will listen closer.

TALK WITH THE EYES

Another quirk that comes from spending the last thirty years in noisy bars: I am an expert eye-roller. If people can't hear me, and I can't hear them, I have to make facial expressions that convey a million different emotions and reactions. I love how fans have picked up on this and put my eye rolls and gestures on continuous two-second loops called GIFs and posted them up all over the Internet. Google *Big Ang GIFs* and you'll see. Cracks me up!

DRINK IT OLD-SCHOOL

People come into the Drunken Monkey and want all kinds of crazy drinks. To keep up with the trends, we came up with a bunch of fruity cocktails. Margo has vague memories of drinks called the Cranky Monkey, the Funky Monkey, the Jumpy Monkey, the Wacked Monkey, Blackout Monkey, Coma Monkey, Incarcerated Monkey, the Rat Monkey. The list goes on, but I don't remember any of the recipes. They were all *horrible*.

My taste is old-fashioned. I don't like these ten-splash-in-a-glass cocktails. Give me my red wine with cream soda on Sunday. A shot of tequila when I'm working. At Christmas, I make a mimosa that's so festive, it's like drinking a freakin' tree. If I go exotic, it's a new twist on an old classic, the martini. My two faves:

THE ESPRESSO MARTINI. Put equal parts Belvedere vanilla vodka and Kahlúa in a shaker with ice and a few fresh-roasted espresso beans. Shake it to death and pour into a chilled martini glass.

THE LYCHEE NUT MARTINI. Put a few ounces of vodka, a splash of vermouth, and an ounce of juice from a jar of lychee nuts into a shaker with ice. Shake it to death, and pour into a chilled martini glass. Garnish with a lychee nut.

HANG AROUND FOR LAST CALL

I usually leave the bar at 4:00 a.m. The street is nearly empty, and hardly any people are around. This is the quiet part of my day, the ten-minute drive from the Drunken Monkey back home. As exhausted as I am, I find myself smiling at what went down that night, and who stopped in. I welcome anyone to come by, to say hello. The bar is not only where I work, it's my second home.

17

Big Fame Rules

ome of my friends say that they always knew I'd blow up one day. If I ever thought that myself, I didn't expect it to happen at fifty-two! I never sought out any kind of fame. I've been too busy supporting my family, enjoying my friends, and trying to have a good time. Of course, being on TV and getting recognized is a huge change. How many fifty-two-year-old, grandma bartenders from Brooklyn turn into TV stars? It's not normal. This is just not how things are supposed to be. Yet, here I am, writing a book about my life. When I finish this chapter, I have to run down to the Drunken Monkey and do a sound check for the reopening-night party, which will be filmed. Then I have to do a radio interview and run to a meeting in Manhattan with my managers and agent.

It's insane—and absolutely fantastic. You will *never* hear

me complaining about being famous. I love this shit! Even when I'm tired, I've got a smile on my face 24–7. People send me gifts. Fans come to the bar from all over the world to say hello and take pictures. I'm getting to meet amazing people and make new friends. Fame has become another way for me to form new relationships. It can last for another fifteen minutes or another fifteen years. I don't care! I'm enjoying it while it lasts and soaking up the positive vibes along the way. Thanks to *Mob Wives* and *Big Ang*, I'm feeling the love from all over the world.

66 Fame hasn't changed Ang one bit. Nothing could change her. She's always been the way she is now. Her persona on TV is exactly the way she is. That's why people love her. You can see that genuineness, the authenticity."

—*Donna, sister*

BE OPEN TO ANYTHING

Here's the story of how I wound up on *Mob Wives*: the show's producer Jennifer Graziano, Celia's niece, called me up and asked, "Hey, Ang, wanna come on my TV show?"

I said, "Why not?" I knew the other girls in the cast and

thought it'd be fun. I'd never done anything like that before. I just went where they told me to go. They filmed me at the bar, at my house, at dinner. They taped for hours. The "pickup" segments when I talk directly to the camera were a lot of fun. I got to glam out for those—full makeup, hair, and outfits. A month or two later, I saw myself on TV. Bam. I know it sounds silly to say, but it happened so fast.

> 66 I've known Big Ang forever, since I was a kid. She is best friends with my aunt Celia and older sister Renee. She's been like a part of my family for thirty years. In Brooklyn and Staten Island, Ang has always been a kind of celebrity. Say her name, people know who you mean, and they smile. So when I was developing *Mob Wives*, I thought about Ang for season one. She was always in the back of my mind, a trick up my sleeve. You don't want to play all your cards right away. So I did season one with the four women, got that established, and then brought in Ang as a secret weapon in season two. The rest is history. She's a huge hit. A breakout. And now, we're filming her spin-off show, *Big Ang*."
>
> —*Jennifer, producer*

" As soon as I heard about Ang coming on the show, I was all for it. And it was the greatest gift that God gave me. She balanced us. She brought in a healthy dose of humor and gave everyone a chance to laugh instead of scream and pull hair. Personally, during the shooting of season two, Ang was a real support through the whole thing with my son's father [cooperating with the Feds]. She never spoke ill and just helped me tremendously. She's helped other people her whole life. And this is her chance to shine."

—Renee, Mob Wives castmate

TREAT EVERYONE WITH RESPECT

Of the thousands of people I've met, I've certainly liked some better than others. The reason they all seem to like me is because I treat everyone the same. From the homeless man on the street to celebrities and wiseguys, they all get my respect and kindness. It's not my style to be a bitch. It's also not my style to look down on anyone, because you never know where they've been, and where they're going. We're all just one good or bad decision away from either being locked up or sitting on a throne.

KEEP IT IN PERSPECTIVE

When good things come later in life, like fame or love, you appreciate it more. If you're young and are cast in the spotlight, it creates a sense of entitlement, like, "I belong here, and I'm going to stay here forever." Then, when the spotlight moves on, you're left in the cold. I don't worry about that. I have perspective about what's happened in my life. I know who I am. The fame doesn't define me. I won't change. I can appreciate the newfound money and attention for what it is: a windfall out of the blue. It's an amazing surprise that I wasn't expecting, or counting on. I know to be grateful for it, and to treasure it for as long as it lasts.

❝ All these years, we've had to deal with people coming up to us in bars and clubs, making comments about her looks. When she walks in, everyone turns their heads. Good or bad, she's always gotten attention. In life, you can't judge someone until you know her. Ang is a wonderful person, and that's what people respond to. And now, her unique style is finally paying off for her. Everyone knows her. Before, it was all over the five boroughs. Now it's all over the world.

"No one deserves this more than Ang. She's not a phony. She's generous and kind. It's good karma coming back to her."

—Angelina, friend

THE NOT-SO-FANTASTIC PART

I'm so freakin' busy! I never get a break. Here's my typical day:

7:00 a.m.: Wake up when Sal jumps in the bed. Get up, make him breakfast, give him a bath, get him dressed, and drive him to school. Do all personal errands, like food and clothes shopping. Clean the house, get dressed.

12:00 noon: Go to the bar and check everything.

2:00 p.m.: Begin filming *Mob Wives* or *Big Ang*. Filming is on and off all day long.

3:00 p.m.: Get Sal at school.

5:00 p.m.: More errands and filming. Maybe get in a treatment or two. Take Louie for a walk.

7:00 p.m.: Make and serve dinner to the family. Clean up after.

9:00 p.m.: Back to the bar until closing.

4:00 a.m.: Fall in bed, exhausted. Do it all over again tomorrow.

I'm not complaining. You can love your life *and* feel exhausted.

The only other drawback to fame is that I can't do some things I used to do without being mobbed. In public, I can't talk on the phone because people are constantly saying, "Is that you?" I'm, like, "Shhh! I'm trying to talk!" I took my niece Sonnie shopping for a birthday present. We went to the local mall and got swarmed. I said, "Sonnie, keep your head down and run!" We were chased out of the mall. That shouldn't happen, unless it's the cops coming after you.

I'm getting used to the crush, though. When I do personal appearances, like at Splash, gorgeous half-naked men surround me. Now that's the opposite of a problem—I wish it on every grandmother!

THE WEIRD PART

At this point, I'm used to a car screeching to a stop, and someone jumping out into traffic to take my picture. But when a fan sent roses to the bar with my picture on each flower, I thought, "Weird." Nice, and the roses were beautiful. But it was strange that someone out there is putting so much time into doing that. A fan also had a caricature of my face tattooed on her body. It's an honor that someone did that. I'm excited and it's flattering. It's crazy, too. As a tattoo addict, I understand that impulse. I've had names tattooed on my body that I regretted almost the second the ink was in. I hope that woman doesn't hate hers in a year.

HAVING A FAMOUS RELATIVE

My sisters and brothers are 100 percent loving my newfound fame. Janine gets to show off her beautiful home and her boutique (which has the cutest clothes for kids on Staten Island) on the show. Raquel and A.J. think it's hilarious I'm on TV. I don't think I could have persuaded A.J. to move back in with me unless it was, in part, to be on the show. Raquel can't appear on camera because of her job as a special ed teacher. Her bosses would rather she not do it. Fine, whatever. And

Sal's father won't let him appear on TV either, which I understand (even though I'd love to show off my gorgeous grandson to millions of people!).

My lifelong friends are thrilled for me, and I'm just as pleased to get them involved with it. Whenever possible, they get airtime on the show. If there's a scene at the bar, at least two of my best pals are there. My friends film scenes at my apartment, just hanging out, cooking and eating. When I go out to dinner on camera, I go to one of my friends' restaurants. I've filmed at Tina's Beyond Beauty Day Spa, at Hollywood Puppy, and at my cousin Sallyann's pool party. I love sharing the spotlight. It comes from the same place as constantly wanting to feed people. It's not enough to enjoy the food myself. I want everyone I know to love it, too. That makes everything all the more delicious.

GIVE BACK

Lately, I've had more opportunities to help good causes. I still do breast-cancer walks in honor of Cari-Ann. I recently did a charity walk for prescription-drug-abuse awareness. My big push last winter was to raise money for a kid from the neighborhood with cancer.

It feels good to do good. I've lived this way my whole life. I'm always giving—gifts, drinks, the shirt off my back, food (obviously)—to my family and friends. Charity begins in the home, and it spills out onto the street. Whenever I see someone in need, I act. Just last week, I was pulling out of the driveway, and I saw this kid from the block collapse on the sidewalk. I jumped out of the car and called 911. I stayed with him until the ambulance came. He came by the house a few days later to explain. Turns out, he was on a new medication and had a bad reaction to it. Only eighteen, and he had a heart attack! All I did was call 911 and show some human kindness and consideration. He said, "You saved my life." Like I could do anything else but help.

I hate to see anyone treated with a lack of compassion. I was in Vincent's Clam Bar on Mott Street in Little Italy a few years ago, and a homeless man with no legs rolled into the place on his wheelchair. The bouncer threw him out like he was garbage. I said, "How can you do that?"

The bouncer said, "He can't stay if he can't pay."

I was horrified. I said, "He's with me, and I'm paying." I grabbed the handles of the chair and said, "Come on."

It was one of the most fascinating dinners I've ever had. The homeless guy, named Gary, said he'd been a lawyer once, but fell on hard times, then health problems, then worse times. I don't know the specifics. He didn't get into the gritty details. He just gave us the basic story, and then we talked about life, enjoyed our lobster, and toasted with champagne. I have no idea if he really was a lawyer. But he was smart and polite and a great talker. You never know what's going to happen in life, good or bad. Anyone can rise and fall, or fall and rise. That's why I treasure my friends, love my family, live as high as I can, soak up the spotlight, stay happy, stay young, eat the lobster, and drink the champagne, as much as I can, for as long as I can.

KEEP ON SURVIVING

Without a doubt, I am most excited about my bar blowing up. You don't even have a clue. I've worked my ass off and watched one bar after the next close down. The Drunken Monkey almost went down the same path. My cousin Sally-ann and I opened the place in 2008 with high hopes and expectations. When the bar was new to the neighborhood, it did okay. We struggled to keep the momentum building and hardly made any money. And then, the recession hit.

Practically overnight, our business died. You'd think people would want to drown their sorrows when times are tough. They did, but they bought their booze at a liquor store and drank it at home. We went from just getting by to hanging on by a thread.

When the chips were down, I did what I've done in the past. I reached out to friends and family and borrowed money to keep the Drunken Monkey up and running (more like crawling). One month, I had to borrow $40,000 to cover expenses. I was getting loans from everyone. To their credit (and my debt), people would write me checks, no question. I am forever grateful for their trust in me, and for believing I could turn things around.

But at a certain point, you have to ask yourself, how much money can I possibly borrow? Was I throwing money that wasn't even mine into a black hole? There had to be a limit. Christmas 2011, we were in sorry, sad shape. I didn't think I could hold on for another month. I wanted to shutter the place. Sallyann said, "Just wait until *Mob Wives* airs. You never know." On New Year's Day, season two premiered.

 " The next day, the bar was packed—I mean *packed*—and it has been every day after. I took home eleven hundred dollars for one night, after bringing home nothing for years. Ang has always been unique. I knew she'd be a millionaire, and that we'd be a success as partners. The success is all the sweeter for having toughed out the rough times."

—*Sallyann, cousin*

That first episode, I got only a few minutes of airtime. Every week, I got a little bit more. I'm writing this only five months after I made my TV debut. I was in debt up to my eyeballs then. And now, I've paid it all back and had enough left over to remodel the bar. We had to make room for the increase in customers!

It's a version of the American survival story. I say survival, not success. That's how I think of it. In the grand scheme of my whole life—fifty-two years of it—I've been on TV for just a blip. For decades before that, I've been a survivor. My newfound fame is just another way I've managed to keep my head up and support my family—they're the reason I've been striving all these years. If this run of good fortune stops, I'll come up with something else.

EPILOGUE
Moving Day

SUNDAY, MEMORIAL DAY
WEEKEND, 2012

We moved into our new house a week ago. It's not finished yet. Dom and his crew are putting new flooring in the connected apartment where Raquel and Sal will sleep (all their waking moments will be in the main house, I'm sure).

A.J. hasn't officially moved out of his Brooklyn apartment yet, but he's packing. Neil and I went to Florida for a week, filming *Big Ang* and kicking back, so the hard-core decorating and furniture shopping has yet to begin.

Today, I'm throwing a party. It is a holiday, after all. I've got a new pool, a Jacuzzi, and an amazing deck with a picnic table that seats twelve. It's eighty degrees and hot for May (thank you, global warming), so everyone's psyched to come over, bob in the pool, drink Twisted Tea and cold beers. Neil isn't much of a cook, but he's pretty good behind the grill, making burgers and hot dogs, chicken and ribs. His daughter is coming, and all my nieces and nephews, aunts, friends, brothers and sisters, cousins. Basically, everyone in the borough is on the way. I'm starving, but I've got only two hours to decide what to wear, pull the house together, and roll about a million meatballs.

As I'm typing this, I realize that my life hasn't changed much in the last six months. It's just another Sunday, and another Sunday dinner. Sure, it's a nicer house. But I'm hosting the same people, cooking my usual specialties. The feeling of making Sunday dinner—rushing around, looking forward to eating and drinking, excited to see everyone—is the same today, at this high point in my life, as it was at the lower points. When people say that fame hasn't changed me, it's because the things I do and the people I do them with haven't changed.

I'm only four years younger than my mom was when she passed away so suddenly. After all these years of trying to live up to her legacy, I can take stock and see that Janine and Dom and I have become the glue that holds our family together, just like Mom used to be. The Sunday dinners are at my house, and people come out of the woodwork to show up. Thank God they do. Without my family, I have no idea where I'd be now. But I sure wouldn't be here in this beautiful house, or as happy.

But I'd probably still be making meatballs.

ACKNOWLEDGMENTS

Thanks to everyone for always being at my side, through it all. I love all of you:

Janine Detore, my sister. Without her, I couldn't have written this book.

Raquel and A.J., my kids.

Neil, my husband.

Dominick, my brother-in-law.

Donna, my sister.

Marianne Donofrio, the best grandmother, and she's like my own mother to me.

Angela, Angelina, Brianna, Celia, Deb, Denise, Jeannie, Jenn, Kevin, Lori, Margo, Renee, Rita, Ronald, Ronnie, Ryan, Sallyann, and Tina, for sharing your stories.

Jennifer Graziano and Marvin Peart, my managers.

Louise Burke, Jennifer Bergstrom, Jeremie Ruby-Strauss, Kate Dresser, and Heather Hunt at Gallery Books.

Dan Strone and Kseniya Zaslavskaya at Trident Media Group.

Valerie Frankel, for helping me put it all together.

Printed in the United States
By Bookmasters